VEGETABLE GENIUS

Anna Berrill is a food writer and editor based in London. She is a regular contributor to *Feast*, the *Guardian*'s Saturday food magazine and writes their weekly Kitchen Aide column. She has previously worked for *Waitrose Food*, *Jamie Magazine*, *Red*, *Homes & Gardens*, *Food & Travel*, the *Huffington Post*, *Healthy* and *Decanter*. She also appeared on Radio 4's *The Food Programme*, as well as the *Guardian*'s *Today in Focus* podcast. This experience has given her a keen eye for food trends, what people are cooking and how to get the best out of each ingredient.

Agnieszka Więckowska is a Polish illustrator and graphic designer based in Wrocław with 15 years' experience in the creative industry. She focuses on creating illustrations for publishers, institutions and brands, including Adobe, Kinley and Accor. szarobiuro.eu

Anna Berrill

VEGETABLE GENIUS

200 CLEVER WAYS TO TAKE YOUR VEGETABLES FURTHER

Illustrations by Agnieszka Więckowska

Skittledog

Contents

Year of the vegetable

This is a book about vegetables: simple ways to put courgettes, mushrooms, kale and the like at the heart of the table. They are the starting point for so many of my meals, but it is impossible to talk about vegetables without mentioning their power to capture a moment or season.

My uncle's garden was like Narnia: a gate, at what appeared to be the end, opened onto trees laden with apples in autumn, carrots peeping from the soil in winter and ladders of runner beans in summer. There was also a greenhouse where cucumbers, tomatoes and marrows grew. Sometimes there was swag to take home, which my mum turned into wonderful things: a kind-of paella, crumble (of course), or – and this was a favourite aged 10 – baked cheesy potatoes crowned with slices of tomato. This seemed worlds away from the produce on Chapel Market in North London, where my mum usually shopped and where you could pretty much find anything all year round.

Vegetables have always been central to the way my family cooks, and now how I cook. But the way I think about them is constantly evolving, with different veg falling in and out of dishes, depending on the season and my mood. There are, of course, those hardworking, dependable vegetables that grease the wheels of weeknight dinners. For me, that's broccoli for one-pot pastas (page 34), kale crisped up and tossed through noodles (page 91), or peas (ideally fresh, but otherwise frozen) thrown into fried rice with prawns and kimchi (page 42).

Then there are the guest stars who appear at different points of the year, and splinter into everything I cook while I've got the chance: sweetcorn to eat on the cob with lashings of spicy lime butter (page 27), tossed into savoury scones (page 27), or bolstering creamy, comforting polenta (page 27); asparagus to combine with eggs and pile onto toast with a sprinkle of garlic crumbs (page 95) because, well, double carbs are always a good idea; broad beans to toss into crab cakes (page 163); or sprouts to stuff inside tacos (page 99), or crown puff pastry with comté and walnuts (page 98).

That said, there are also the lurkers, those vegetables suffering something of a PR problem. Swede, for example, doesn't often grace my shopping list, but it is ideal for roasting with sausages, apples and maple syrup (page 106), or mashing to finish a harissa-spiked shepherd's pie (page 107). Turnips, meanwhile, add pep to one of my favourite comfort foods, dal (page 62), and can, in general, be used where you would a potato – Spanish tortillas (page 63) are a great example.

The world is really your vegetable, but, of course, they will always be at their most flavourful when picked at the right time of year: hardy kale in cooler times, asparagus in spring and tomatoes in late summer. That said, life is always better when sweet tomatoes are at hand, so it's eminently sensible to want to feel their love in the winter dearth, too. Knocking up a big batch of, say, roast tomato and miso sauce (page 154), something to preserve and conserve for the months ahead, is just good sense. And on the subject of tomatoes, you'll notice I've taken a loose approach to the term 'vegetable'. Yes, I know aubergines and tomatoes are technically fruit, but in my mind, they are worthy of their spot here; so many of my meals would be at a loss without their presence in sauces.

Prep your veggies like a pro

Vegetables are inherently flexible and can elevate so many dishes to delicious heights – if you treat them right, that is.

KEEP YOUR COOL

When it comes to storing veg, you want to keep your fridge between 3°C and 5°C, and don't pack it to the rafters – the air needs to be able to circulate so your fridge works at its optimum efficiency. The top shelf should be reserved for things like cooked veg, prepared salads, dips, cucumber and cheese (wrapped in wax or greaseproof paper and popped in a container ideally lined with kitchen towel). Store mushrooms on the middle shelf as the ethylene they produce will cause other things to ripen and spoil, and remember fungi don't like plastic, so house them in paper bags or cardboard punnets. Raw meat and fish should be kept on the bottom shelf, as well as anything you're defrosting from the freezer. Then to the vegetable drawer (or crisper), where most of your vegetables, salad, fresh herbs and lettuces will live. Potatoes and root veg should go into dark, breathable bags, while the likes of pumpkins and tomatoes like to be kept at room temperature. Ultimately, though, you need to keep tabs on what's in your fridge, so keep older veg near the front for visibility.

MAKE FRIENDS WITH YOUR FREEZER

Preserving aside, a glut of vegetables can also be frozen. In general, they need to be blanched first: drop into boiling water for 1–3 minutes (depending on the vegetable), then remove and plunge into ice-cold water to prevent further cooking. Of course, not all vegetables can be frozen, with kale, lettuce, cucumber and Jerusalem artichokes being examples of those that cannot.

USE THE WHOLE INGREDIENT

Be sure to make use of the entire vegetable (think leaves, stalks) where possible. Potato skins, for example, will add flavour to soups; parsnip tops can be snipped and added to salads or soups; carrot tops, meanwhile, are ideal for pounding into pesto. And if you've got a surplus of veg or they're on the turn, look to chutneys, pickles and ferments, such as kimchi or sauerkraut. You'll just need a good heavy-based saucepan and some sterilized jars – do this by washing them in hot, soapy water, rinsing well, then drip-drying upside down before transferring to an oven at 100°C (80°C fan)/gas ½ for 20 minutes. If you're making jam, you'll also want some saucers to pop in the freezer for 15 minutes for the set test (spoon the hot jam onto the plate, then push your finger through it – if it wrinkles, it's ready).

AND ALWAYS KEEP THINGS INTERESTING

The joy of vegetables is really the copious ways in which they can be cooked: steaming, frying, roasting, charring (to name but a few). If you're in a cooking rut, shake things up by switching technique or using a completely different veg. Craving mash? Swap potatoes for sweet potato, carrot or swede. Or if you're after a rosti, use parsnips instead.

THE KIT LIST

When cooking with vegetables, there are some essential tools that will just make life easier.

Knives A good chef's knife (as large as you feel comfortable holding) plus a petty knife/small utility knife or paring knife.

Y-shaped vegetable peeler Besides peeling skins, I also use this to ribbon courgettes and shred cabbage for slaws.

Microplane zesters A game changer for fine citrus zest, but also garlic, ginger, cheese and nutmeg.

Mandolin Perfect for thin slices of veg, but be warned: these aren't for the accident-prone.

Pestle and mortar For grinding spices and pounding pestos.

Steamer basket Can also be used to steam dumplings.

Offset spatula For spreading pastes or spices onto veg and getting into all the nooks and crannies of pans and bowls.

Dough scraper Not a silicone or metal one (it has to be plastic). Will ensure bowls and surfaces are clean of sticky veg-laden doughs for loaves or scones.

Glass storage containers They clean well, won't stain and are ideal for storing leftovers (and even reheating food).

Digital scales and measuring spoons Essential for accuracy.

Chopping boards They must be wooden (they'll last forever).

Mixing bowls A few in different sizes are advisable. Ditch the plastic wrap and store wet or crumbly mixtures in a deep bowl covered by a plate.

Stick blender For soups, marinades, sauces and curry pastes.

Food processor For chopping veg, whizzing super-smooth dips or pumpkin falafel (page 39).

Fluted tart tin A 23cm tin is useful for savoury tarts and quiches.

Good-quality roasting trays and pans You only really need three pans in your arsenal: a cast-iron frying pan, a casserole dish and a smaller saucepan.

Courgette

One of summer's most abundant vegetables (well, technically, courgettes are fruit). Their subtle flavour lends itself to a variety of dishes and applications, from grilling, roasting and stewing, to baking into muffins or loaf cakes. As courgettes cook, their flavour intensifies, moving from mellow to sweet and, if the heat is high, the flesh becomes wonderfully creamy, too. Courgettes can turn their hand to both comfort (creamy lasagnes, risottos or cut into fries) and lighter and brighter things (roasted for a couscous salad, chopped into salsa, grated for fritters). But in either case they like something sour, whether that's vinegar (think red wine) or a good squeeze of lemon juice.

SEASON	Early summer to early autumn
PAIR WITH	Prawns, crab, lamb, bacon, peas, tomatoes, potatoes, artichokes, cheese (feta, ricotta, halloumi, goat's cheese), lime, white beans, chilli, harissa, tahini, basil, mint, hazelnuts, pine nuts, cumin.
HACK	To caramelize this water-rich veg, you'll need a flat baking sheet and a hot oven, otherwise it'll just steam in its own juice.

Courgette, cheese and chive soda bread

2 large courgettes (about 400g), grated
200g wholemeal spelt flour, plus extra for dusting
200g white spelt flour
1½ tsp bicarbonate of soda
60g rolled oats
100g cheddar, grated
20g chives, snipped
300ml buttermilk
Oil, for brushing

While this does keep for a few days, soda bread is best eaten on the day of baking, which really is no hardship.

Put the grated courgettes in a bowl, sprinkle with salt and leave for 15 minutes; squeeze out as much water as possible. In a bowl, combine the flours, bicarb, oats and a pinch of salt. Toss in the courgettes with your hands, breaking them up, then stir in the cheese and chives. Stir in the buttermilk then tip onto a baking tray sprinkled with flour and quickly shape into a round loaf. Lightly brush with oil, then score a deep cross on the top. Bake at 180°C (160°C fan)/gas 4 for 35-40 minutes until golden. (To check it's ready, tap the bottom - it should sound hollow.) Cool before slicing. Makes 1 loaf.

Kind-of courgette carbonara

200g tagliatelle
1 tsp olive oil
100g diced pancetta
2 courgettes, ribboned
2 garlic cloves, finely chopped
60g parmesan, grated
Half a lemon, zested and juiced

A lighter carbonara-inspired pasta, which still brings all the comfort and joy of the classic. A scattering of parsley leaves to finish would be nice.

Cook the pasta in salted boiling water according to packet instructions, then drain reserving a mugful of pasta water. Meanwhile, heat the oil in a frying pan, then add the pancetta and fry for 5 minutes. Add the courgettes and continue cooking for 5 minutes until soft. Stir in the garlic, cook for another minute, then season. Toss in the pasta, then sprinkle over the parmesan, lemon zest and juice and a splash of pasta cooking water. Toss again, adding more pasta water if it's dry. Serves 2.

Courgette, mint and halloumi burgers

2 courgettes, grated
100g halloumi, grated
4 spring onions, finely chopped
Large handful mint leaves, finely chopped
1 lemon, zested
80g dried breadcrumbs
Large pinch of chilli flakes
1 egg

Light, veg-laden burgers to stuff inside buns with a load of chilli jam.

Put the grated courgettes in a bowl, sprinkle with salt and leave for 15 minutes; squeeze out as much water as possible. In a large bowl, combine the courgettes with the remaining ingredients and season well. Shape into four large or six small patties, transfer to a lined baking tray and chill in the fridge while you heat the oven to 220°C (200°C fan)/gas 7. Bake for 20 minutes, until crisp and golden. Makes 4-6.

Courgette agrodolce and ricotta flatbreads

3 tbsp olive oil
1 red onion, finely sliced
2 garlic cloves, sliced
2 large courgettes (about 400g), sliced
Half a lemon, zested and juiced
Large pinch of saffron
Pinch of chilli flakes
2 tbsp toasted pine nuts
2 tbsp sultanas
Large handful mint leaves, sliced
1 tbsp sherry vinegar
120g ricotta
2 flatbreads

This sweet-sour way with courgettes is so easy and an Italian classic. It also keeps well in the fridge, so make in advance for a speedy weeknight dinner.

Heat the oil in a heavy-based pan and gently cook the onion, garlic and a pinch of salt for 10 minutes. Add the courgette slices, lemon zest, saffron and chilli and cook down until the veg have completely softened – about 15 minutes. Turn off the heat, stir through the pine nuts, sultanas, mint, lemon juice and vinegar. Heat the grill to high and put the flatbreads on a baking tray. Season the ricotta with salt and pepper, then divide between the flatbreads and spread to cover each base. Top with the courgettes and grill for 5 minutes. Makes 2.

Harissa hasselback courgettes with spiced hazelnut crumble

2 courgettes
2 tsp harissa
3 tsp olive oil
Good squeeze of lemon juice
1 small garlic clove, crushed
½ tsp ground cumin
10g pine nuts
1 tsp coriander seeds
½ tsp cumin seeds
10g blanched hazelnuts

To make cutting the courgettes easier, put the veg between the handles of two wooden spoons (this will stop the knife cutting all the way through).

Put the courgettes on a chopping board and make vertical slices all the way along each one at 3mm intervals – you want the slices to go three-quarters of the way through. Combine the harissa, oil, lemon juice, garlic and some salt and pepper, then massage into the courgettes. Roast at 200°C (180°C fan)/gas 6 for 30-40 minutes, until soft. Meanwhile, in a mortar, crush the remaining ingredients together. Serve the courgettes sprinkled with the hazelnut crumble. Serves 2 as a side.

Radish

Plump, hot, crunchy radishes are prime for pinching whenever the fridge is opened. I usually eat them raw – with cool, salted butter or sliced in salads and slaws – but they also respond well to heat, whether roasted or sauteed, with their texture softening and their peppery nature mellowing. I'm partial to the white-tipped ones, but radishes come in a mix of colours, from pink to purple. It's best to trim the leaves from the radish, as they draw out moisture, and store them separately.

SEASON	Late spring to mid-autumn
PAIR WITH	Pork, mackerel, butter, eggs, beetroot, cucumber, lettuce, spring onions, new potatoes, citrus, peanuts, miso, soy sauce, preserved lemon.
HACK	For extra crispness, dunk radishes and their leaves in iced water for an hour before using.

Radish and watermelon salad

500g watermelon, sliced
200g radishes, sliced
50g rocket
2 tbsp olive oil
1 lime, juiced
Handful mint leaves, sliced
50g feta, crumbled

Sweet, refreshing watermelon works really well in salads, particularly when paired with bitter radishes.

Put the watermelon, radishes and rocket in a bowl, toss with the olive oil and the lime juice and some salt and pepper. Tip onto a plate and top with the mint leaves and feta. Serves 4-6.

Miso butter radishes

20g unsalted butter
1 tbsp white miso
500g radishes, halved
1 tsp honey
Half a lime

A simple, speedy side which packs a punch. Serve with salmon or a Sunday roast.

Put the butter, miso and radishes in a saucepan over a medium heat and toss to coat. Once the butter has melted, add 1 tbsp water then cover and cook for 5 minutes, or until the radishes are tender. Stir through the honey and a good squeeze of lime juice. Serves 4.

Pickled radishes

150ml white wine vinegar
Half a lemon, juiced
1 tsp salt
50g sugar
300g radishes, halved
5 sprigs dill, thick stems
  discarded

Some sliced root ginger would make a very nice addition to this pickle.

Put the vinegar, lemon juice, 50ml water, salt and sugar in a pan and bring to the boil. Put the radishes and dill in a sterilized jar then pour over the hot liquid. Pop the lid on and leave to cool, then transfer to the fridge for 2 days before opening. Serves 4.

Roast radishes with preserved lemon

For added crispiness, leave the radish leaves on the roots.

400g radishes,
  large ones halved
1 garlic clove, chopped
1 preserved lemon, flesh
  discarded, rind finely
  chopped
Drizzle of olive oil
Large handful parsley,
  chopped

Combine the radishes, garlic, preserved lemon and oil in a baking dish with a pinch of salt and roast at 200°C (180°C fan)/gas 6 for 30 minutes, stirring halfway through. Remove from the oven and stir through the parsley. Serves 2-4.

Curried egg, radish and potato salad

This can be made the day before and kept in the fridge, ready for lunch boxes.

400g new potatoes, halved
3 spring onions, chopped
3 hard-boiled eggs,
  chopped
6 radishes, sliced
2 tbsp olive oil, plus extra
  for drizzling
5 curry leaves
½ tsp ground cumin
½ tsp ground coriander
2 large handfuls watercress

Put the potatoes in a pan, cover with water, add a pinch of salt and bring to the boil. Cook until tender, then drain and leave to cool. Transfer the potatoes to a serving bowl and add the spring onions, eggs and radishes. Heat the oil in a pan, then add the curry leaves, cumin and coriander and cook until fragrant, about 30 seconds. Pour the lot over the potato mix and season with salt. Add the watercress and toss well. Serve drizzled with a little more oil. Serves 4-6.

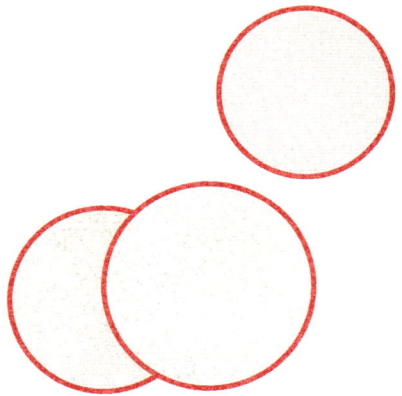

Green beans

When it comes to green beans, I don't like to discriminate and use French and runner interchangeably. Crunchy and bright, they are one of summer's most accommodating vegetables: blanch, grill, steam, saute with oil and salt, slow cook with tomatoes, or simply stir into curries and soups. That said, green beans do rub along particularly well with salty, briny things, so it's always a good idea to pair them with capers, olives and the like.

SEASON	Green beans: late summer to early autumn; runner beans: early summer to late autumn
PAIR WITH	Tuna, anchovies, prawns, chicken, paneer, tomatoes, radishes, shallots, garlic, chilli, ginger, parmesan, feta, olives, capers, lemon, mustard, honey, soy sauce.
HACK	When faced with a glut, make dilly beans: place some garlic, dill and dried chilli into sterilized jars, then pack in the green beans upright. Bring equal amounts of white wine vinegar and water to the boil with some salt, then pour over the beans. Seal and pop in a hot water bath for 10 minutes. Leave for a week before eating with cheese.

Tomato and green bean spelt

2 tbsp olive oil
1 shallot, chopped
2 garlic cloves, chopped
200g green beans,
    trimmed and halved
400g cherry tomatoes,
    roughly chopped
2 tbsp tomato puree
500ml stock
200g spelt
Tahini, to drizzle (optional)

If you have any tahini, it's worth stirring a drizzle through this nutty, chewy spelt dish. It really lightens things up.

Heat the oil in a large pan, add the shallot, garlic and green beans and cook for 2 minutes. Add the tomatoes, season with salt and pepper and cook for another 15 minutes. Stir in the tomato puree, tip in the stock and spelt and simmer for another hour, adding a splash of water if it starts to look dry. Drizzle with tahini, stir and serve. Serves 2 as a main, 4 as a side.

Paneer with green beans

½ tsp ground turmeric
½ tsp ground cumin
½ tsp ground coriander
200g paneer, cut
    into cubes
Oil
1 tsp cumin seeds
½ tsp black mustard seeds
1 red onion, chopped
2 garlic cloves, chopped
Thumb-sized piece of
    ginger, chopped
1 green chilli, chopped
400g tin chopped
    tomatoes
200g green beans,
    trimmed
30g natural yoghurt
    (a big spoonful)

Served with rice or bread, this makes a satisfying weeknight meal.

In a bowl, combine the turmeric, ground cumin, coriander and a pinch of salt, then add the paneer and toss to coat. Heat a glug of oil in a pan and cook the paneer on each side until golden; set aside. In the same pan, add a little more oil, then toast the cumin seeds and black mustard seeds until they start to pop. Add the onion, garlic, ginger and chilli and cook for 10 minutes. Tip in the tomatoes, add a pinch of salt and cook for another 10 minutes, before stirring in the green beans, paneer and 100ml water. Simmer for 10 minutes, then turn off the heat and stir through the yoghurt. Serves 2 as a main, or 4 as part of a spread.

Lemony beans with oregano

3 tbsp olive oil
1 onion
2 garlic cloves, chopped
150g cherry tomatoes, halved
300g green beans, trimmed
Half a lemon, zested and juiced
1 tsp dried oregano

A good squeeze of lemon will bring the whole thing to life, so this is not the moment to be reserved.

Heat the oil in a large heavy-based pan, add the onion and cook for 10 minutes. Stir in the garlic, cook for a minute, then add the tomatoes, beans, lemon zest, oregano and some salt and pepper. Tip in 2 tbsp water and cook for 25 minutes, adding a splash more water if things start to stick. Add a good squeeze of lemon juice and combine. Serves 2–3.

Gado gado

250g new potatoes
150g green beans, trimmed
1 large carrot, cut into matchsticks
Half a cucumber, thickly sliced
3 hard-boiled eggs, halved

FOR THE SAUCE
1 garlic clove, chopped
1 red chilli, chopped
Oil
120g peanut butter
2 tbsp lime juice
1 tbsp kecap manis
½ tsp brown sugar

Swap the vegetables, depending on your preference and what you have in. Radishes, beansprouts, broccoli and Chinese cabbage all work well.

Fry the garlic and chilli in a little oil until softened, about 4 minutes, then transfer to a blender with the remaining sauce ingredients and a pinch of salt. Pulse, then add 50ml water and pulse again; you're looking for a pourable consistency, so add a splash more water if need be. Cook the potatoes in a pan of salted boiling water until tender, about 10 minutes, adding the beans for the last few minutes. Drain then transfer to a plate with the carrot, cucumber and eggs. Spoon over some of the sauce and serve with the rest of the sauce on the side. Serves 4–6.

Green beans with dill and mustard

400g green beans, trimmed
3 tbsp olive oil, plus extra for drizzling
2 tsp Dijon mustard
1 lemon, juiced
Handful dill, chopped
½ tbsp white wine vinegar

You can use whatever herbs take your fancy, be it parsley or even mint.

In a large bowl, toss the beans with a good drizzle of oil and some salt and pepper. Heat a frying pan, then tip in the beans and cook, turning occasionally, for 5 minutes. In a bowl, whisk together the mustard, lemon juice, olive oil, dill and vinegar. Toss the beans and dressing together. Serves 4.

Sweetcorn

Cooking with sweetcorn simply feels fun, whether that's down to the Jolly Green Giant commercials for the tinned stuff, or gnawing on whole corn cobs held by those wooden corn holders on their yearly outing. Sweet and juicy, sweetcorn just tastes of summer, although it does tip into the start of autumn, so the fresh stuff can also mean more warming chowders, curries and ramens, as well as lighter salsas, muffins and burgers.

SEASON	Late summer to mid-autumn
PAIR WITH	Chicken, bacon, haddock, salmon, prawns, tomatoes, spring onions, avocado, parmesan, cheddar, chilli, lime, coriander, mayonnaise, honey, coconut, peanuts.
HACK	Every part of a corn cob is usable. Empty cobs bring a subtle flavour to stock, so try adding them to the next risotto you make.

Sweetcorn and peanut butter soupy noodles

Quick and satisfying – the ultimate bowl food.

800ml stock

Handful coriander, stems finely chopped, leaves set aside

1 green chilli, finely chopped

1 spring onion, finely chopped

2 garlic cloves, finely chopped

Thumb-sized piece of ginger, finely chopped

1 tsp rice wine vinegar

1 tsp soy sauce

1 tbsp peanut butter

120g ramen noodles

Kernels sliced from 2 corn cobs

80g sugar snap peas, halved on the diagonal

Handful of beansprouts

Pour the stock into a large pan and add the coriander stalks, chilli, onion, garlic, ginger, vinegar, soy sauce and peanut butter. Bring to a simmer and let it bubble away for 5 minutes. Add the noodles and cook according to packet instructions, adding the corn for the last 3 minutes. Stir in the sugar snap peas and spoon into two bowls. Garnish with beansprouts and the coriander leaves Serves 2.

Lemony sweetcorn and ricotta fusilli

Summer pasta is the best kind of pasta, especially when the sauce can be made in the time it takes to boil your carbs. If you don't have fresh sweetcorn, use tinned.

200g fusilli

1 tbsp olive oil

1 garlic clove, chopped

½ red chilli, chopped

150g sweetcorn kernels

1 lemon, zested, plus the juice of half

60g ricotta

Large handful basil, leaves torn

Cook the pasta in salted boiling water according to packet instructions. Meanwhile, heat the oil in a large pan cook the garlic and chilli for a minute, then add the sweetcorn and lemon zest and continue cooking for 5 minutes. Drain the pasta, reserving a mugful of cooking water. Tip the pasta into the sweetcorn pan, then stir in the ricotta, lemon juice and a splash of cooking water to loosen. Season and stir through the basil. Serves 2.

Corn on the cob with lime and chilli

4 corn cobs
80g butter, softened
1 red chilli, finely chopped
1 lime, zested and juiced
Handful coriander leaves,
  to serve

If the weather isn't on your side, ditch the barbecue and do this in a griddle pan.

Heat the barbecue and, once hot, cook the corn, turning occasionally, for 30 minutes until charred in places. Meanwhile, mix the butter, chilli, lime zest and juice with a pinch of salt. When the corn is cooked, smear with the butter and serve scattered with coriander leaves. Serves 4.

Cheddar, chilli and sweetcorn scones

Kernels sliced from
  2 corn cobs
300g self-raising flour,
  plus extra for dusting
1 tsp baking powder
½ tsp salt
70g butter, cubed
6 spring onions, finely
  sliced
130g cheddar, grated
130ml milk, plus extra
  for brushing

These scones are wonderfully cheesy and ideal served warm with lots of butter, or on the side of some soup.

Cook the sweetcorn kernels in salted simmering water for 5 minutes; drain. In a large bowl, combine the flour, baking powder and salt, then rub in the butter until you have fine crumbs. Stir in the corn, onion and cheese, then fold in the milk. Tip out onto a lightly floured worktop and knead slightly. Stamp out into about ten rounds, then transfer to a lined baking tray. Brush with milk and bake at 220°C (200°C fan)/gas 7 for 12 minutes until risen and golden. Makes 10.

Corny polenta

500ml stock
100g quick-cook polenta
Kernels sliced from
  2 corn cobs
20g butter
50g parmesan, grated

Sweet and soothing, this is crying out to be topped with some greens or something saucy.

Pour the stock into a large pan and bring to the boil. Tip in the polenta and corn and stir constantly until cooked and thick. Season with black pepper and stir in the butter and parmesan. Serves 2.

Chard

These wonderfully robust and sharp, fan-like leaves can do it all, taking the lead in tarts, pies or gratins, or playing more of a supporting role, stirred by the handful of deep plumes into soups or stews. Rainbow chard is a riot of colour, with bright light stems in red, white and yellow (destined to be braised or baked with eggs); while Swiss chard has broader, flatter white stems, with glossy leaves (good for gratins, curries and stuffing inside toasties). You can use them pretty much anywhere you would spinach, but chard very much likes to collide with cheese (comté, ricotta, feta, parmesan).

SEASON	Early summer to late autumn
PAIR WITH	Cod, bacon, lamb, squash, celeriac, tomatoes, mushrooms, lemon, olives, miso, walnuts, mustard, cheese (see above), tamarind.
HACK	Don't ditch chard stems: chop and cook with onion, carrot and celery to start soups and stews; alternatively, cook them slowly in meat or veg stews, or pickle them.

Buckwheat galettes with mushrooms and chard

Top with a fried egg for the perfect weekend brunch.

100g buckwheat flour
1 egg, beaten
250ml milk
Olive oil
250g mushrooms, sliced
1 garlic clove, chopped
200g chard leaves,
  chopped
Half a lemon, zested
40g butter
80g cheddar, grated

In a large bowl, whisk the flour and beaten egg with a pinch of salt. Slowly whisk in the milk, then set aside. Heat a little oil in a pan, then add the mushrooms and a pinch of salt and cook for 6 minutes. Add the garlic, cook for a minute, then add the chard leaves and lemon zest, and continue cooking until the leaves have wilted. Season with black pepper and remove from the heat. Melt the butter in a frying pan, then tip into the batter and combine. Return the frying pan to the heat and ladle in a quarter of the batter, swirling it around so it reaches the edges. Cook over a high heat until golden underneath - about 2 minutes. Flip, continue cooking for 2 minutes, then add a quarter of the cheese in the middle, followed by a quarter of the chard mix. Fold up the sides of the pancake so you have a square and continue cooking for 1 minute. Repeat with the remaining batter and filling. Serves 4.

Chard farinata

This chickpea pancake is great for sharing but be warned: farinata doesn't keep, so this is one to eat straight away.

250g gram flour
Olive oil
2 garlic cloves, sliced
200g Swiss chard, stems
  cut into 1cm pieces,
  leaves roughly chopped
1 tsp fennel seeds
1 tsp baking powder
Grated parmesan, to serve

In a large bowl, combine the flour with a large pinch of salt. Make a well in the middle, pour in 450ml water and whisk until you have a batter. Cover and set aside for at least 2 hours. Meanwhile, heat 1 tbsp oil in a pan, add the garlic and cook for a minute. Add the chard stems and fennel seeds, cook for a few minutes until softened, then add the leaves and continue cooking until wilted. Season. Whisk 2 tbsp oil and the baking powder into the batter, then pour onto a baking tray lined with greaseproof paper that has been brushed with oil. Top with the chard and bake at 240°C (220°C fan)/gas 9 for 15-20 minutes, until golden. Serve with a grating of parmesan. Serves 6.

Chard with saffron and almonds

30g almonds
2 tbsp olive oil
1 large onion, thinly sliced
400g Swiss chard, stems cut into 2cm pieces, leaves torn
2 garlic cloves, chopped
Large pinch of saffron
100ml stock
1 tbsp lemon juice

Of course, this is great served warm, but it can also sit for a while and be eaten at room temperature.

Toast the almonds in the oven at 200°C (180°C fan)/gas 6 for 8 minutes. Set aside to cool, then chop. Heat the oil in a pan, then add the onion and some seasoning, and cook for 5 minutes until softened. Add the chard stems, cook for 5 minutes, then stir through the garlic and saffron, and cook for a minute. Pour in the stock and simmer for a few minutes, then add the chard leaves and continue cooking until wilted. Stir in the lemon juice, then serve topped with the almonds. Serves 4 as a side.

Cheesy baked polenta and chard

1 tbsp olive oil
250g chard, stems cut into 2cm pieces, leaves sliced
1 tsp chopped thyme
Pinch of chilli flakes
1 garlic clove, sliced
600ml stock
100g quick-cook polenta
25g parmesan, grated

This is pure comfort and destined to be eaten in bowls on the sofa.

Heat the oil in a large pan, then add the chard stems and a pinch of salt and cook for 5 minutes. Stir in the thyme, chilli and garlic, cook for a minute, then add the chard leaves and continue cooking until wilted. Meanwhile, pour the stock into another pan and bring to a simmer. Whisk in the polenta, lower the heat and cook, whisking continuously, until thickened. Stir in the parmesan and some black pepper, then spoon onto a baking tray. Top with the chard and bake at 200°C (180°C fan)/gas 6 for 15 minutes. Serves 2.

Chard, sweet potato and peanut stew

1 tbsp oil
1 onion, roughly chopped
2 garlic cloves, chopped
1 red pepper, chopped
200g rainbow chard, leaves and stems chopped
Pinch of chilli flakes
1 tsp cumin seeds
1 tsp coriander seeds
2 tbsp peanut butter
400ml stock
3 sweet potatoes, cut into bite-sized chunks

Quinoa would make a fine base for this creamy, comforting stew.

Heat the oil in a large pan, add the onion, garlic, pepper, chard stems and chilli and cook until softened, about 10 minutes. Add the cumin and coriander seeds, peanut butter and stock, and bring to a simmer. Add the sweet potato, cover and cook for 30 minutes until the potatoes are cooked through. Stir in the chard leaves and cook until wilted, then season. Serves 4.

Broccoli

Ever since I discovered the simple joy of broccoli pasta, this brassica has been a constant companion – florets boiled in well-salted water are added to a pan of olive oil, garlic and chilli and cooked until the greens break up and become almost creamy. Broccoli's ability to soak up flavour is unrivalled, which is why it pays to go punchy (soy sauce, chilli, anchovies, for example) and keep the heat high (grill, char, fry, roast). As well as calabrese, there's sprouting broccoli, with its purple heads signalling spring is coming; and long, bright Tenderstem and broccoli rabe, aka the perfect partner to pasta. It really is a failsafe start to most dinners.

SEASON	Mid-autumn to mid-spring
PAIR WITH	Prawns, anchovies, sausages, 'nduja, bacon, tofu, cheese (cheddar, stilton, parmesan, ricotta, goat's cheese), watercress, peas, kale, chilli, yuzu, lime, miso, soy sauce, tahini, white beans.
HACK	Don't forget the broccoli stalks: chop up and cook with your florets or thinly slice and dunk into hummus.

Salmon, broccoli and noodle traybake

Thumb-sized piece of ginger, grated
1 small garlic clove, grated
2 tsp sesame oil, plus extra for the noodles
3 tbsp soy sauce
1 tsp honey
2 tsp rice vinegar
2 nests of dried egg noodles, cooked
200g Tenderstem broccoli
2 skinless salmon fillets
Handful coriander leaves
1 spring onion, finely sliced
Half a lime

Here, I like to keep the broccoli crunchy. If you prefer it on the softer side, pop it in the oven with the noodles and sauce for 5 minutes before putting the salmon on top.

In a bowl, combine the ginger, garlic, sesame oil, soy sauce, honey and rice vinegar. Tip the cooked noodles onto a baking tray, drizzle with oil and cook in the oven at 210°C (190°C fan)/gas 6½ for 5 minutes. Remove the tray from the oven, add the broccoli, pour over the sauce and toss everything together. Pop the fish on top and return to the oven for 20 minutes, until the salmon is cooked through. Scatter over the coriander leaves and spring onion, then squeeze over the lime juice. Serves 2.

One-pot broccoli orzo

3 tbsp olive oil
3 garlic cloves, finely sliced
1 broccoli crown, separated into florets and stems, chopped
Half a lemon, zested and juiced
Pinch of chilli flakes
200g dried orzo
600ml vegetable stock
15g parmesan, grated, plus extra to serve
Handful basil, torn

Broccoli pasta is the perfect carb comfort and this one-pot version saves on the washing-up, too.

Heat 2 tbsp oil in a large pan. Add the garlic, broccoli stems, ½ tsp salt and a generous amount of black pepper. Cook for 5 minutes. Add the broccoli florets, lemon zest and chilli flakes and continue cooking, stirring occasionally, until softened, about 5 minutes. Tip in the orzo then toast, stirring for a minute. Stir in the stock and parmesan, bring to the boil. Lower the heat and simmer, covered and stirring occasionally, until the pasta is al dente, 8-10 minutes. Remove from the heat, then stir through the lemon juice and 1 tbsp olive oil. Stir in the basil and serve with more grated parmesan. Serves 2.

PSB with romesco, pine nuts and sultanas

30g sultanas
450g jar roasted red peppers, drained
1 tsp paprika
80g blanched almonds
1 tbsp sherry vinegar
2 garlic cloves: 1 peeled, 1 finely sliced
4 tbsp olive oil
200g purple sprouting broccoli
40g toasted pine nuts

This blend of roasted red peppers and almonds goes wonderfully with the garlicky broccoli. Serve with good hunks of bread.

Put the sultanas in a small bowl, cover with just-boiled water and leave to soak. Put the peppers, paprika, almonds, vinegar and whole garlic clove in a food processor and blitz to a paste. With the motor still running, drizzle in 3 tbsp olive oil. Season and spoon onto a large plate. Heat the remaining 1 tbsp olive oil in a frying pan, add the sliced garlic and cook on low until golden and crisp. Meanwhile, cook the broccoli in salted boiling water for 4 minutes until tender then drain. Toss the broccoli in the garlic oil, stir in the sultanas and pine nuts, then spoon the lot over the romesco. Serves 4 as a side.

PSB, goat's curd and pumpkin seed pesto sandwiches

Crisp yet tender broccoli, creamy goat's curd and a textured pesto all in fluffy focaccia - everyone needs a good sandwich in their lunch arsenal.

200g purple sprouting broccoli

50ml olive oil, plus extra for roasting

¼ tsp garlic granules

50g pumpkin seeds, toasted

1 small garlic clove, peeled

10g basil

10g parsley

30g parmesan

Half a lemon

Focaccia

150g goat's curd or soft goat's cheese

Put the broccoli in a roasting tin, drizzle with oil, sprinkle over the garlic granules and season. Toss well, then roast at 240°C (220°C fan)/gas 9 for 15 minutes, until charred. Meanwhile, in a food processor, pulse the pumpkin seeds, garlic and a pinch of salt. Add the herbs and pulse again until you have a paste. Stir in the parmesan, 50ml olive oil and a squeeze of lemon, then taste and adjust if needed. Slice wedges of focaccia in half, then spread the bases with a layer of pumpkin seed pesto. Top with the broccoli, followed by the goat's curd. Serves 2-3.

Broccoli, lemongrass and ginger fried 'rice'

Here, broccoli is blitzed to resemble rice then fried with lots of aromatics, ready to be crowned with a fried egg.

1 broccoli crown, stem finely chopped, florets divided

1 shallot, diced

2 garlic cloves, crushed

Thumb-sized piece of ginger, finely chopped

1 red chilli, finely chopped

1 lemongrass stalk, finely chopped

Drizzle of sesame oil

2 tbsp soy sauce

2 tbsp lime juice

Drizzle of honey

2 spring onions, finely chopped

Coriander leaves, to serve

Fried eggs, to serve (optional)

Blitz the broccoli stem in a food processor until it resembles rice, then transfer to a bowl; do the same with the florets. In a heavy-based pan, cook the shallot, garlic, ginger, chilli and lemongrass in a little sesame oil until softened, about 10 minutes. Add the broccoli and cook until softened. Stir in the soy sauce, lime juice and honey, then spoon into bowls and garnish with the spring onions and coriander. Topping with a fried egg would be a good idea. Serves 4 as a side.

Pumpkin

It's impossible to separate pumpkins from Halloween. There was
a time they were solely reserved for carving and putting on the
doorstep, but nowadays, I appreciate their glowing flesh for other
reasons, bringing pumpkins in from the cold to add to soups
and curries, pies and cakes. Granted, they do require a bit of
work breaching the thick skin, and a fair bit of seed-scooping and
chopping of their fibrous flesh. But the rewards are great, especially
when roasted with olive oil and salt, or just put in the oven *au naturel*
in chunks (skin and all) until collapsed, then blended to a puree
ready to kick off cakes and cookies, pies and pancakes.

SEASON	Mid-autumn to early winter
PAIR WITH	Prawns, salty cheese, bacon, lemon, chilli, coconut, miso, radicchio, rosemary, sage, lemongrass, ginger, walnuts, pecans, cinnamon, cardamom, nutmeg, chocolate.
HACK	Roasting pumpkin seeds is a no-brainer; flavour with things like harissa, curry powder, cinnamon, soy sauce. Be sure to clean the seeds properly, though. The best way to do this is to soak them in water to remove the membrane.

Pumpkin puree

800g pumpkin

This is the starting point of so many recipes, from dips to bakes, which is why I've kept things nice and simple. Happily, this makes enough to make both the pancakes and dip below.

Cut the pumpkin into quarters, then scoop out the seeds. Transfer the quarters to a lined baking tray, flesh-side up, and roast at 180°C (160°C fan)/gas 4 for 45 minutes, until completely soft. Once cool enough to handle, scoop out the flesh and blitz in a blender until you have a puree. This will keep in the fridge for a couple of days; alternatively, store in the freezer for up to 3 months.

Pumpkin pie pancakes

100g plain flour
½ tsp baking powder
½ tsp bicarbonate of soda
1 tbsp caster sugar
1 tsp ground cinnamon
½ tsp ground ginger
100g pumpkin puree
2 eggs
280ml buttermilk
1 tsp vanilla extract
Butter, for cooking

A real taste of autumn, drizzled with maple syrup and scattered with blueberries.

In a large bowl, combine the dry ingredients. In a second, combine the pumpkin and other wet ingredients. Tip the wet mix into the dry, combine, and set aside for 10 minutes. Heat a little butter in a frying pan, swirling around to cover the base. Working in batches, place dollops of pancake mix in the pan and fry for 3-4 minutes, then flip and continue cooking on the other side for 2 minutes until crisp. Makes 8-10.

Pumpkin, cumin and tahini dip

200g pumpkin puree
1 garlic clove, chopped
570g jar chickpeas, drained
2 tbsp tahini
Half a lemon, juiced
½ tsp paprika
½ tsp ground cumin
2 tbsp olive oil

Adding an ice cube is the key to a beautifully whipped dip. Serve with crudites and crisps.

Put all the ingredients apart from the oil in a blender. Add an ice cube and blitz until smooth. With the motor still running, trickle in the oil. Season. Serves 8.

Stuffed pumpkin with wild rice

This is a great autumn sharing dish, which just so happens to be vegan. The wild rice adds an earthy aroma to the sweet pumpkin. Serve in wedges.

1 pumpkin
300g wild rice
1 litre hot vegetable stock
1 tbsp olive oil, plus extra
  for rubbing
1 onion, diced
1 leek, diced
1 garlic clove, crushed
50g dried cranberries
1 tbsp wholegrain mustard
Big handful parsley,
  chopped

Use a small knife to cut off the pumpkin lid, then scoop out and discard the seeds and stringy bits. Rub the inside of the pumpkin with a bit of salt and set aside on a lined baking tray. Put the rice in a saucepan, pour over the stock and simmer, stirring occasionally, until the rice is cooked – about 30 minutes. Meanwhile, heat the oil in a pan and cook the onion and leek until softened. Add the garlic, cook for another minute, then take off the heat and stir in the cranberries, mustard, parsley and cooked rice. Spoon the rice mix into the pumpkin, squashing it down. Pop the lid on and rub the pumpkin all over with oil. Cook in the oven at 200°C (180°C fan)/gas 6 for 1 hour, or until a knife easily goes through the pumpkin. Serves 6.

Baked pumpkin falafel

Pile into pitta with a drizzle of tahini and a crunchy salad (shredded red cabbage would work particularly well).

500g pumpkin,
  peeled and diced
Olive oil
400g jar or tin chickpeas,
  drained
2 garlic cloves, chopped
1 tsp cumin seeds
2 tsp coriander seeds
Big pinch of chilli flakes
½ tsp bicarbonate of soda
Big handful parsley
3 tbsp gram flour

Put the pumpkin in a baking tray, drizzle with oil and season. Toss to coat, then bake at 200°C (180°C fan)/gas 6 for 20 minutes, until tender. Turn the oven up to 220°C (200°C fan)/gas 7. Transfer the pumpkin to a food processor with the chickpeas, garlic, spices, bicarb, parsley and some seasoning. Blitz until smooth, then transfer to a bowl. Stir in the flour, then form into ten patties. Transfer to a lined baking tray, drizzle with oil and bake for 25 minutes. Makes 10.

Peas

Peas are a constant in my life; they were housed in the freezer all year round ready to accompany the likes of sausages as we were growing up, but more likely these days they're popped from their pods in summer to toss through salads, pastas and risotto. The sweet, humble pea is incredibly versatile: blanch and crush with oil and chilli to top flatbreads (ideally with poached eggs), turn into fritters or add to frittatas. When fresh, though, there really is no better idea than getting a load of peas in their shells on the barbecue until nicely charred, then tossing with good olive oil, herbs and salt and eating like edamame.

SEASON	Late spring to late summer (turn to the frozen ones the rest of the year)
PAIR WITH	Bacon, chicken, pork belly, crab, salmon, prawns, cod, feta, goat's cheese, burrata, eggs, spinach, courgettes, spring onions, potatoes, romaine lettuce, chilli, lemon, mint, tarragon, coconut, hazelnuts.
HACK	Small but mighty, peas are a source of fibre, magnesium and iron, as well as protein.

Pea and kimchi rice with prawns

1 tbsp sesame oil
3 spring onions, chopped
2 garlic cloves, chopped
Thumb-sized piece of
  ginger, chopped
100g peas
2 tbsp kimchi, chopped
1 tsp gochujang
150g peeled raw prawns
100g jasmine rice, cooked
  and cooled
Splash of soy sauce
Sesame seeds, to serve

This really benefits from an egg, so soft boil a couple, slice them in half and nestle on top.

Heat the sesame oil in a frying pan, then cook the spring onions, garlic and ginger for a couple of minutes. Tip in the peas, kimchi and gochujang, cook for 2 minutes, then add the prawns and cook for another 2 minutes. Tip in the cooked rice, breaking it up with a spoon, and continue cooking until the prawns are cooked and the rice heated through, about 2 minutes. Add a splash of soy sauce, then serve with a scattering of sesame seeds. Serves 2.

White bean primavera

10g butter
1 tbsp olive oil
1 leek, chopped
150g asparagus, cut into
  2cm pieces
100g peas
100ml stock
50ml white wine
325g jar white beans,
  drained
Half a lemon, zested,
  plus a squeeze of juice
2 handfuls spinach
Handful basil leaves, torn
Parmesan, to serve

Primavera is a dish that's full of hope, utilizing all the spring veg. Be sure to add a good squeeze of lemon at the end for extra brightness.

Heat the butter and oil in a large pan then, once the butter has melted, add the leek and cook for 5 minutes. Add the asparagus and peas, cook for another 10 minutes, then pour in the stock and wine. Simmer until the liquid has almost all evaporated, then season. Stir in the beans, lemon zest and spinach and continue cooking until the spinach has wilted and the beans are warmed through. Stir through the basil and a squeeze of lemon juice, then serve topped with parmesan. Serves 2.

Pea and preserved lemon dip with halloumi dunkers

300g peas
1 garlic clove, chopped
1 preserved lemon, flesh
  discarded, rind finely
  chopped
Big handful mint leaves
Half a lemon, juiced
Pinch of chilli flakes
2 tbsp olive oil, plus extra
  for frying
200g halloumi, cut into
  fingers

Swap crackers and crudites for halloumi to dunk in this zippy dip.

Cook the peas in a pan of salted boiling water until tender; drain and transfer to a blender. Add the remaining ingredients, except the halloumi, season with salt and pepper and blitz – you still want a bit of texture here. Transfer to a bowl. Heat a little oil in a non-stick frying pan, then fry the halloumi on each side until golden. Serves 4.

Crushed pea flatbreads with chilli crisp eggs

With its warm heat and incredible depth of flavour, crispy chilli oil makes everything taste better (but particularly fried eggs).

200g peas
Handful coriander, leaves chopped
Half a lemon, zested, plus a squeeze of juice
2 tsp sesame oil
2 tsp crispy chilli oil
2 eggs
2 flatbreads
1 spring onion, finely sliced

Cook the peas in salted boiling water until tender; drain and transfer to a bowl. Mash with a pinch of salt, then mix in the coriander, lemon zest and juice; set aside. Put a non-stick frying pan over a medium heat, add the sesame oil and crispy chilli oil and give the pan a swirl. Once hot, crack in the eggs and season with salt. Cook until the whites are set to your liking (for me, that's 4–5 minutes). Heat the flatbreads, spoon over the pea mix and top with the chilli eggs. Drizzle over the oil from the pan then scatter over the spring onion. Serves 2.

Pea, spinach and broad bean triangles

Peas and broad beans mingle with the flavours of spanakopita in these hand-held filo pies.

1 onion, finely chopped
2 garlic cloves, finely chopped
1 tbsp olive oil
200g peas
100g broad beans
2 large handfuls spinach, chopped
80g feta
Large handful mint, leaves chopped
1 preserved lemon, flesh discarded, rind finely chopped
4 sheets of filo
Large knob of butter, melted
Sesame seeds, to scatter

In a large pan, fry the onion and garlic in the oil until soft. Add the peas and beans, cook until tender, then stir through the spinach until wilted and any liquid has evaporated. Tip the lot into a bowl, crumble in the feta and add the mint, lemon rind and a generous grind of black pepper. Cut a filo sheet into three strips and brush with melted butter. Put 2 tbsp pea mixture at the top of one strip, fold diagonally to form a triangle, then keep folding down. Repeat with the rest of the mixture and filo. Brush each triangle with more butter, sprinkle with sesame seeds and bake at 180°C (160°C fan)/gas 4 for 20–25 minutes until golden. Makes 12.

Aubergine

Technically a berry, but treated as a vegetable, the aubergine is often misunderstood. Despite its bad rep for squeaking upon eating and having bitter skin, when cooked correctly – whether that's roasted to the verge of collapse, fried, grilled or steamed – it yields a wonderfully silky, creamy texture. And it takes on all the flavour of whatever it's cooked with, so this is the time to make the most of your spice rack, those punchy sauces, or simply some good, peppery olive oil.

SEASON	Summer
PREP	First, don't prep aubergines long before you want to cook, because the flesh can discolour. If you're not cooking aubergines whole, trim off the green calyx at the top before slicing, dicing or cutting into chunks. Some say salting the flesh before cooking will reduce bitterness, but nowadays its main purpose is to draw out excess liquid.
HACK	Swap your packet of crisps for a baked aubergine version. Slice thinly into discs, place in a bowl with some salt, combine and leave for half an hour. Mix with olive oil, grated parmesan, some herbs and seasoning, then bake in a single layer at 200°C (180°C fan)/gas 6 for 15 minutes, turning once, until golden and crisp.

Aubergine cannelloni

2 aubergines
Olive oil
50g parmesan, grated
Handful basil leaves,
  finely chopped
1 red onion, chopped
3 garlic cloves, chopped
½ tsp fennel seeds
1 tsp dried oregano
400g tin chopped
  tomatoes
200g dried cannelloni
  tubes

Here, I've used dried cannelloni tubes, but you could roll fresh lasagne sheets into tubes instead.

Slice the aubergines into rounds, drizzle with oil and griddle on both sides until soft; you will need to do this in batches. Chop the aubergine finely and combine with 40g of the cheese, most of the basil and some seasoning. Put 2 tbsp olive oil in a pan and cook the onion until softened. Stir through the garlic, cook for a minute, then add the fennel, oregano and some seasoning. Tip in the tomatoes, plus half a tin of water. Bring to a simmer and cook for 10 minutes. Spoon some sauce into the base of a baking dish. Fill the cannelloni with the aubergine mix, lay them on top of the sauce, then tip over the remaining sauce. Sprinkle with the remaining cheese and basil and bake at 200°C (180°C fan)/gas 6 for 30 minutes. Serves 4.

Aubergine kedgeree

1 aubergine,
  cut into chunks
Oil
½ tsp ground turmeric
2 eggs
1 onion, chopped
1 tsp curry powder
½ tsp ground coriander
800ml vegetable stock
300g basmati rice, rinsed
  under cold water
Half a lemon, juiced
Large handful coriander
  leaves, chopped

While kedgeree is usually made with smoked fish, it also works well with turmeric-roasted aubergine.

Put the aubergine in a roasting tin and toss with a drizzle of oil, the turmeric and some salt and roast at 200°C (180°C fan)/gas 6 for 15 minutes. Meanwhile, cook the eggs in a pan of salted water for 7 minutes, then transfer to a bowl of cold water to stop them cooking further. Cook the onion in a drizzle of oil in a pan for 5 minutes, then stir in the curry powder and ground coriander and cook for another minute. Tip in the stock, bring to a simmer, then add the rice and cook, covered, for 15 minutes; set aside for 10 minutes with the lid still on. Fluff the rice with a fork, then stir through the aubergine and a good squeeze of lemon juice. Peel and chop the eggs, then add them with the coriander leaves. Serves 2.

Aubergine raita

1 aubergine
Quarter of a cucumber
150g natural yoghurt
Small handful mint leaves, chopped

It is best to cook the aubergine on a barbecue or over the open flame of a gas hob to get a smoky flavour. Alternatively, cut in half, drizzle with oil and pop under the grill until blistered.

Char the aubergine on a barbecue or directly over the flame of a gas hob, using tongs to turn it, until soft and charred. Once cool enough to handle, cut in half, scoop the flesh into a colander and leave to drain for 30 minutes. Grate the cucumber, squeeze out the water, then transfer to a bowl. Chop the aubergine and add to the cucumber bowl with the yoghurt and a pinch of salt. Stir in the mint. Serves 4.

Aubergine satay wedges

100g peanut butter
1 tbsp soy sauce
1 tbsp honey
Pinch of chilli flakes
Small thumb-sized piece of ginger, grated
1 small garlic clove, crushed
50ml coconut milk
1 lime, juiced
3 aubergines, cut into wedges
Oil

If you have any crispy fried onions in the cupboard, sprinkle some over the cooked wedges.

Combine the first six ingredients in a bowl, then stir in the coconut milk and lime juice. Taste and adjust as needed. Put the aubergine wedges on a baking tray, drizzle with oil, add a pinch of salt and toss well. Roast at 220°C (200°C fan)/gas 7 for 30 minutes. Pour over the sauce, then return to the oven for 5 minutes. Serves 4-6.

Spiced aubergine and chickpea stew

1 tbsp olive oil
1 onion, chopped
2 garlic cloves, chopped
2 small aubergines, cut into chunks
1 tsp cumin seeds, crushed
1 tbsp tomato puree
2 tbsp rose harissa
400g tin chopped tomatoes
400g tin chickpeas
Half a lemon, juiced
Handful parsley leaves

A soothing stew to pile into bowls with a good dollop of natural yoghurt.

Heat the oil in a large pan, then add the onion and garlic and cook, stirring occasionally, for 10 minutes. Add the aubergines, cumin, tomato puree, harissa and a pinch of salt and cook for 5 minutes. Tip in the chopped tomatoes, cook for 10 minutes, then tip in the chickpeas (including their liquid) and bring to a simmer. Cook for 15 minutes, until the tomatoes have thickened and the aubergine is soft. Season, then add a good squeeze of lemon juice and the parsley. Serves 2-3.

Cauliflower

This is the social friend of the vegetable world, whose mild flavour plays well with all manner of spices, herbs and heavy-hitting sauces and condiments (think soy, miso, tahini). Cauliflower is also versatile to boot: grate it to make rice or pizza bases, blitz into bolognese, fritters or soups, mash it to top pies, cut into florets for curries and tacos, or simply treat it like a piece of meat, marinating and roasting, grilling or burying in the pit of a barbecue. It will stand up to every one of these techniques.

SEASON	Late winter to late spring; late summer to early winter
PREP	Trim the leaves, then you have options: either remove the hard inner core and separate the individual florets (if your cauliflower is large, cut the florets up), slice into 3–4cm steaks through the stem, or remove the base of the core (so it stands flat) and leave whole ready to roast.
HACK	Cauliflower freezes well. To do this, blanch florets in boiling water, drain and plunge into ice-cold water. Drain again then transfer to freezer bags and seal.

Cauliflower tacos with cashew crema

1 red onion, very finely sliced

3 limes, juiced

Pinch of dried oregano

1 cauliflower

3 garlic cloves; 2 crushed, 1 roughly chopped

2 tbsp harissa

1 tsp dried thyme

2 tbsp olive oil

150g cashews, soaked in water for 2 hours

Tacos, to serve

The nuts need to be soaked in water for a couple of hours, but the finished crema can be kept in the fridge for up to a week.

Put the onion in a bowl, add a good pinch of salt and stir; set aside for 10 minutes. Squeeze over the juice of 2 limes, add a pinch of oregano, combine and set aside again. Cut the cauliflower into florets and tip into a baking tray. In a small bowl, combine the crushed garlic, harissa, thyme, the juice of the remaining lime, the olive oil and a pinch of salt. Tip over the cauliflower, combine and roast at 220°C (200°C fan)/gas 7 for 30 minutes, stirring halfway through. Meanwhile, make the crema: drain the cashews, then put in a food processor with 100ml water, the chopped garlic clove and a pinch of salt and pulse smooth. Heat the tacos then smear with the crema. Top with the cauliflower and pickled onions. Serves 2.

Chard, tapenade and cauliflower tart

1 large cauliflower, broken into florets

1 egg, beaten

25g parmesan, grated

2 garlic cloves: 1 crushed, 1 finely chopped

5g oregano sprigs, leaves picked and chopped

1 tbsp olive oil

1 onion, sliced

150g chard, leaves torn, stems chopped into 2cm pieces

90g black olive tapenade

Pinch of chilli flakes

Tarts don't have to mean pastry. Here, cauliflower is blitzed and bound with egg and cheese to make a light vehicle for the topping.

Blitz the cauliflower florets in a food processor until the mixture resembles couscous (you may need to do this in batches), then tip into a large bowl. Add the egg, parmesan, crushed garlic and oregano and combine. Tip onto a baking tray lined with greaseproof paper and flatten with your hands into a disc. Cook in the oven at 200°C (180°C fan)/gas 6 for 25 minutes. Meanwhile, heat the oil in a large pan, then add the onion, chard stems and some salt and pepper and cook for 10 minutes. Stir in the chopped garlic, cook for 1 minute, then add the chard leaves and continue cooking until wilted. Spread the tapenade over the cooked base and spoon over the chard mix. Scatter with chilli flakes and return to the oven for 15 minutes. Serves 4.

Cauliflower tabbouleh

1 cauliflower, broken into florets

Half a lemon, juiced

3 tbsp olive oil

1 tbsp za'atar

1 spring onion, chopped

Large handful mint, chopped

Large handful parsley, chopped

For more of a meal, stir through chopped cucumber, tomatoes, crumbled feta, pomegranate seeds, or chopped toasted pistachios.

Blitz the cauliflower florets in a food processor until the mixture resembles couscous (you may need to do this in batches), then tip into a large bowl. Add the lemon juice and 1 tsp salt, stir and leave for 30 minutes. Add the olive oil, za'atar, spring onion, herbs and a generous grind of black pepper and combine. Serves 4.

Roast cauliflower and peanut curry

1 cauliflower, broken into small florets

400g tin chickpeas, drained

1 tsp ground cumin

Coconut oil

1 red onion, finely chopped

2 garlic cloves, finely chopped

Knob of ginger, finely chopped

1 red chilli, finely chopped

Small bunch coriander, leaves picked, stems chopped

3 tbsp peanut butter

2 tbsp soy sauce

1 lime, juiced

200ml coconut milk

Large handful spinach

Cauliflower and peanut butter are great friends in this creamy curry, which needs little more than some flatbreads for mopping.

Tip the cauliflower, chickpeas, cumin, 1 tbsp coconut oil and some salt and pepper into a roasting tin. Toss well then roast at 200°C (180°C fan)/gas 6 for 30 minutes. Heat 1 tsp oil in a large pan and cook the onion for 10 minutes. Add the garlic, ginger, chilli and coriander stalks and cook for 5 minutes. In a bowl, combine the peanut butter, soy sauce and lime juice, then tip into the pan with the coconut milk, 50ml water and the roast cauliflower and chickpeas. Simmer for another 5 minutes, then stir through the spinach to wilt. Serve scattered with the coriander leaves. Serves 2 as a main, or 4 as part of a larger spread.

Whole roast cauliflower cheese

1 large cauliflower

50g butter

50g plain flour

550ml whole milk

1 tsp mustard

½ tsp paprika

125g cheddar, grated

Handful parsley leaves, chopped

Everyone's favourite side, roasted whole to serve as a centrepiece. Mix things up by accessorizing with bacon or leeks, or a spoonful of harissa.

Remove any larger leaves from the cauliflower, then lower stem-side up into a pan of salted boiling water. Cook for 10 minutes, then drain and leave to steam dry. Meanwhile, heat the butter in a pan over a medium heat until frothy, then stir in the flour and cook until you have a sandy paste – about 3 minutes. Gradually stir in the milk, cook for 10 minutes until thickened, then stir in the mustard and paprika. Turn off the heat, stir in 100g cheddar and season. Put the cauliflower in the middle of an ovenproof dish, then pour over the sauce and sprinkle with the remaining cheese. Bake uncovered at 200°C (180°C fan)/gas 6 for 30 minutes, until bubbling. Serve scattered with parsley. Serves 6.

Mangetout

Peas, in all their forms, just please. But these crisp, sweet garden ones, which are picked when young, are incredibly handy: slice raw and toss into noodle salad, or steam, boil or stir-fry whole in soups, curries and beyond – after all, mangetout in French means 'eat it all'. My absolute favourite of their characteristics, though, is the crunch, and there is no better showcase for this than rolled in rice paper alongside asparagus, lettuce, vermicelli and copious herbs (coriander, mint) to make summer rolls, to dip into peanut sauce.

SEASON	Early summer to early autumn
PAIR WITH	Beef, pork, salmon, prawns, smoked trout, cucumber, fennel, peppers, pak choi, peas, sweetcorn, coconut, lime, lemongrass, cashews, papaya, hoisin, sumac, peanut butter.
HACK	Mangetout freeze well. If you're faced with a glut, blanch and freeze in portions for future dinners.

Coconut fish with mangetout and lime

Brown rice is the perfect foil to soak up all the golden juices.

Oil
1 onion, grated
1 garlic clove, grated
Thumb-sized piece of
   ginger, grated
1 red chilli, grated
1 tsp ground turmeric
1 tsp ground coriander
1 tsp ground cumin
200ml coconut milk
350g white fish,
   cut into chunks
150g mangetout
1 lime, juiced
Large handful
   coriander leaves

Heat a good glug of oil in a large pan, then add the onion, garlic, ginger and chilli, and cook until softened, about 5 minutes. Stir in the spices, cook for a minute, then pour in the coconut milk and 50ml water. Simmer for 5 minutes, then add the fish and mangetout and simmer for another 10 minutes, until the fish is cooked through. Stir in the lime juice and coriander leaves. Serves 2.

Harissa chicken with green couscous

The meat really benefits from being left to marinate in the fridge for at least 2 hours, or overnight.

2 tsp harissa
2 tsp honey
1 small garlic clove, crushed
4 skin-on, bone-in
   chicken thighs
120g couscous
200ml stock
100g mangetout
Handful mint leaves,
   chopped
Handful parsley, chopped
2 spring onions, sliced
1 lemon, zested and juiced
1 tbsp olive oil

Mix the harissa, honey and garlic in a bowl, then add the chicken thighs, tossing to coat well. Cover and put in the fridge for a couple of hours. Transfer the chicken to a roasting dish, then bake skin-side up at 200°C (180°C fan)/gas 6 for 35 minutes, or until the skin is crisp and the meat is cooked through. Rest for 10 minutes. Meanwhile, put the couscous in a large heatproof bowl and pour over the stock, cover and set aside for 12–15 minutes. Blanch the mangetout for 2 minutes in boiling water, then drain and refresh under cold water. Slice the mangetout then stir through the cooked couscous with the herbs, spring onions, lemon zest and juice, olive oil, and a good grind of black pepper. Serve alongside the chicken. Serves 2.

Macaroni greens

A green version of the classic mac 'n' cheese.

100g frozen peas
100g mangetout, halved
200g dried macaroni
1 garlic clove, chopped
1 tsp olive oil
20g parmesan, grated
Half a lemon, zested and juiced
20g basil

Blanch the peas and mangetout in salted boiling water for 2 minutes. Drain then transfer to a food processor. Meanwhile, cook the macaroni in salted boiling water according to packet instructions, then drain, reserving a mugful of cooking water. Add the garlic, olive oil, cheese, lemon zest and basil to the blender, along with 4 tbsp pasta cooking water. Pulse until you have a sauce, adding more pasta cooking water if needed, then season. Return the pasta to the pan over a low heat, then tip in the sauce, adding a good squeeze of lemon juice, plus a splash more pasta water to loosen if needed. Serves 2.

Green tea rice with mangetout

I drink *a lot* of green tea. Here, cooking the rice in the tea adds a subtle, smoky flavour, which is very welcome.

300g jasmine rice
700ml brewed green tea
Oil
Small bunch spring onions, sliced
2 garlic cloves, crushed
Thumb-sized piece of ginger, chopped
250g mangetout, sliced
1 tbsp soy sauce
½ tbsp rice wine vinegar
Sesame seeds, to serve

Rinse the rice under cold running water, then transfer to a saucepan. Pour over the green tea and season. Bring to the boil, cover and simmer for 10-12 minutes, until the liquid has been absorbed. Leave to stand (still covered) for 10 minutes. Meanwhile, add a glug of oil to a frying pan and cook the spring onions, garlic and ginger for 5 minutes. Add the mangetout, soy sauce and vinegar, and continue cooking for 4 minutes. Stir the veg through the rice and serve scattered with sesame seeds. Serves 4.

Thai green curry

Pile onto jasmine rice and serve with lime wedges on the side.

1 tbsp oil
200g skinless and boneless chicken thighs, cut into bite-sized pieces
Thumb-sized piece of ginger, grated
2 tbsp Thai green curry paste
200ml coconut milk
100g mangetout, halved
1 red pepper, sliced
Half a lime, juiced
Big handful coriander leaves
2 spring onions, sliced

Heat the oil in a large pan, then fry the chicken until golden, about 5 minutes. Add the ginger and curry paste, cook for 2 minutes, then tip in the coconut milk and 100ml water, and simmer for 10 minutes. Add the mangetout and pepper, cook for 3 minutes more, then add the lime juice and coriander. Serve scattered with the spring onions. Serves 2.

Onion

White, red, shallots... Where would we be without onions? Peeling then slicing or dicing onions is the starting point for most dishes, then cooking in a pan with oil, sometimes butter (or both), until sweet and mellow. You then have a base for all sorts, from soups, stews and sauces to curries, as they mingle so well with others. Onions can also be baked, perhaps with butter and herbs, plus a bit of water or stock, or, if they're red, balsamic vinegar and something sweet like maple syrup. Red onions are also acceptable raw, finely sliced with salt and vinegar, sometimes lime juice or spices, for a quick pickle.

SEASON	All year round
PAIR WITH	Sausages, chicken, anchovies, eggs, beetroot, potatoes, cheddar, blue cheese, parmesan, thyme, rosemary, sage, miso... pretty much everything.
HACK	Keep onion skins for making a big pot of stock, ready for soups, stews and risottos.

Miso shallots with polenta

This is pure comfort: meaty onions and all their juices piled onto cheesy polenta.

5 banana shallots, halved
Olive oil
750ml stock
½ tbsp white miso
125g quick-cook polenta
Knob of butter
30g parmesan, grated
2 sprigs thyme, leaves
  picked

Heat the oven to 200°C (180°C fan)/gas 6. Put the shallots in a large roasting tin, drizzle with oil, season with salt and black pepper and toss to coat. Put in the oven for 30 minutes. Meanwhile, combine 150ml stock with the miso. When the shallots have had their 30 minutes, pour the miso stock into the tin, cover with foil and return to the oven for 15 minutes. For the polenta, tip the remaining stock and the polenta into a pan and stir continuously while cooking for 5 minutes. As it thickens, add the butter, parmesan, a good grind of black pepper and the thyme. To serve, spoon the polenta onto plates then top with the shallots and some of their liquid. Serves 2.

Lemony sumac onions

These onions pep up so many things, from salads and sandwiches to grilled meats and fish.

2 tbsp olive oil
2 large red onions,
  finely sliced
2 garlic cloves, chopped
2 tsp sumac
Half a lemon

Heat the oil in a pan over a medium heat, then add the onions and a pinch of salt and cook until completely softened, about 15 minutes. Stir in the garlic, cook for another minute or two, then stir in the sumac and a good squeeze of lemon juice. Taste and add more lemon juice, if needed.

Pork chops and potato boulangère

2 onions, sliced
4 sprigs thyme,
  leaves picked
1 tbsp olive oil,
  plus extra for rubbing
1kg floury potatoes,
  finely sliced
400ml stock
2 pork chops
Handful sage leaves,
  roughly chopped

All this needs is a good spoonful of apple sauce. If, however, you wanted to make this into more of a meal, use 4 small pork chops and serve with cabbage.

Fry the onions, thyme and a pinch of salt in the oil for 10 minutes. Meanwhile, take a baking dish and layer the base with potatoes. Spoon over some onions, then repeat the layers until the potatoes and onions have been used up. Pour over the stock, season and put in the oven at 190°C (170°C fan)/gas 5 for 1 hour. Rub the chops with a little oil, press the sage leaves on them and season. Nestle them into the potatoes and bake for 20 minutes, then turn the chops over and cook for another 20 minutes, until cooked through. Serves 2.

Cheese and onion toasties

Large knob of butter,
  plus extra for spreading
1 tbsp olive oil
4 small onions, sliced
5 sprigs thyme,
  leaves picked
60g cheddar, grated
50g gruyère, grated
4 slices sourdough
Marmite, for spreading

This is a bit like French onion soup wrapped up in a toastie. It's worth weighing the sandwiches down (with a tin, say) when cooking, so they're crisp on the outside and gooey on the inside.

Put the butter and oil in a frying pan and heat until the butter has melted. Add the onions and a pinch of salt and cook for 30 minutes, stirring occasionally. Add the thyme and some black pepper. Combine the two types of grated cheese in a bowl. Slather two slices of the bread with butter (or mayonnaise), then turn them over and spread with a good layer of Marmite. Top the Marmite with the onions followed by the cheese, then pop a second slice of bread on top. Wipe the frying pan clean, then heat. Add the sandwiches and cook until golden on both sides and molten inside, about 4 minutes per side. Makes 2.

Onion and ale gravy

Knob of butter
1 tbsp olive oil
2 white onions, sliced
2 red onions, sliced
2 sprigs thyme,
  leaves picked
100ml ale
300ml stock

A simple yet satisfying gravy to serve with sausages or the sweet potato and red onion toad on page 142.

Melt the butter and oil in a large frying pan, then cook the onions, thyme and a pinch of salt for 45 minutes, until caramelized. Pour in the ale and stock and simmer for 10 minutes. Serves 4.

Turnip

Mellow, bitter turnips perhaps don't have the same allure as potatoes but, generally speaking, you can use them in much the same way. And just like their purple shoulders on a white, rotund body, turnips will add oomph to gratins, tartiflette, soups and stews. Perhaps my favourite way of all, though, is to pan-fry them; something magical happens here and they become wonderfully sweet and juicy, which is particularly good alongside the likes of duck.

SEASON	Mid-autumn to late winter
VARIETIES	Besides winter turnips, there are also baby turnips (available in June and July), which are smaller and sweeter in flavour. They don't require peeling, and are ideal for use in salads.
PAIR WITH	Duck, pork chops, salmon, leeks, carrots, potatoes, apples, kimchi, harissa, miso, honey, mustard, parmesan, chives, coriander.

Turnip and shiitake cake

100g rice flour
1 tbsp cornflour
½ tsp caster sugar
Sesame oil
1 shallot, chopped
1 garlic clove, chopped
300g turnips, grated
1 tbsp soy sauce
100g shiitake mushrooms, chopped

Traditionally, this Chinese dim sum dish is made with daikon, but here I combine turnips and shiitake. You can make this in advance and store in the fridge, ready to fry in slices.

In a large bowl, whisk the flour, cornflour, sugar, 1 tsp sesame oil, a large pinch of salt and 200ml water; set aside. Heat a glug of oil in a saucepan, then cook the shallot until softened. Stir in the garlic, cook for a minute, then add the turnips and soy sauce and cook for 8 minutes. Add the mushrooms and once cooked through, set aside to cool. Once cool, stir the veg into the batter, then transfer to a greased high-sided baking tin (mine was 23 × 30cm). Cover with foil and place in a larger tin. Pour enough boiling water into the larger tin to come three-quarters of the way up the sides of the turnip tin. Bake at 230°C (210°C fan)/gas 8 for 45 minutes, then set aside to cool. Transfer to the fridge to chill for an hour, or overnight. Cut into slices, then fry in oil until golden on each side. Serves 4–6.

Turnip and apple dal

Coconut oil
1 small red onion, grated
1 garlic clove, grated
Thumb-sized piece of ginger, grated
½ tsp ground cumin
½ tsp ground turmeric
Pinch of chilli flakes
100g dried red lentils
200ml coconut milk
300ml stock
300g turnips
1 apple
Half a lime, juiced

Apple brings a nice hit of sweetness to this comforting dal. Crumble poppadoms on top for a bit of crunch.

Heat a little oil in a heavy-based pan, then add the onion, garlic and ginger, and cook for 10 minutes. Stir in the cumin, turmeric and chilli, and cook for another minute until fragrant. Tip in the lentils, coconut milk and stock, and bring to a simmer. Grate the turnips and apple then stir them into the dal and cook for 25 minutes. To finish, stir through the lime juice and a good grind of pepper. Serves 2, or 4 as part of a spread.

Turnip, feta and parsley tortilla

2 tbsp olive oil
1 onion, finely sliced
300g turnips, finely sliced
6 eggs
Large handful parsley,
  chopped
100g feta, crumbled

Eat warm or at room temperature with a dollop of aioli.

Heat the oil in an ovenproof frying pan, then add the onion and cook until softened. Add the turnips, season and cook over a low heat for 30-35 minutes, until the turnips are translucent. Beat the eggs with a pinch of salt in a bowl. Add the parsley, then pour over the turnips and scatter over the feta. Cook for about 5 minutes over a low heat, until the bottom and sides are set. Put under a hot grill for 2 minutes until the top is cooked, then rest for a few minutes before slicing. Serves 4.

Marmalade turnips

1 tbsp oil
2 onions, cut into eighths
Thumb-sized piece of
  ginger, chopped
1 bay leaf
150ml stock
1 tbsp marmalade
1 cinnamon stick
2 star anise
500g turnips, halved

Turnips and orange are perfect partners, which is why marmalade works so well here.

Heat the oil in an ovenproof pan on the hob, then add the onions, ginger and bay, and cook until softened - about 10 minutes. Pour in the stock then stir through the marmalade and spices. Add the turnips, stir to coat well, then bake in the oven, covered, at 180°C (160°C fan)/gas 4 for 25 minutes. Season and serve. Serves 4-6.

Cauliflower and turnip curry with lemon yoghurt

Coconut oil
1 tsp black mustard seeds
10 curry leaves
1 red onion, finely chopped
Thumb-sized piece of
  ginger, grated
Pinch of chilli flakes
2 garlic cloves, chopped
1 tsp ground turmeric
200g tomatoes, chopped
300g turnips, cut into
  small chunks
1 cauliflower, broken into
  small florets
50g natural yoghurt
Squeeze of lemon juice
10g coriander, leaves torn

This is a dish to eat scooped up with flatbreads, although jasmine rice would make a fine alternative.

Heat a little oil in a large frying pan, then add the mustard seeds and curry leaves and cook until the mustard seeds start to pop. Add the onion, ginger, chilli and garlic and cook until softened, about 6 minutes. Stir in the turmeric, cook for a minute, then tip in the tomatoes, turnips, 400ml water and a pinch of salt, and simmer for 10 minutes. Add the cauliflower and simmer for 15 minutes. Meanwhile, in a small bowl, combine the yoghurt, lemon juice, coriander and a pinch of salt. Serve the yoghurt on the side of the curry. Serves 2-4.

Spinach

This leafy green is my weeknight hero, with a handful adding vibrancy as well as nutrients (spinach contains good amounts of fibre, potassium and vitamin A). And it's easy being green: stir through soups, stews and stir-frys to wilt, bake encased in pastry, or serve with eggs. Baby spinach, which is harvested while still young, is smaller and has a milder flavour, making it ideal for serving raw in salads and smoothies or stirring through sauces and curries at the last minute. A bag of the frozen stuff is really worth having too, ready to add to soups straight from the freezer.

SEASON	Late spring to early winter
PREP	Always give spinach a wash before using as the leaves trap sandy soil. Remove any tough stalks.
PAIR WITH	Bacon, sausages, crab, anchovies, sweet potatoes, tomatoes, courgettes, mushrooms, chilli, ginger, watermelon, ricotta, feta, paneer, harissa, chickpeas, cumin, oregano, walnuts.

Homity jackets

The delicious flavours of a classic homity pie stuffed inside a double-baked potato.

2 baking potatoes
2 tbsp olive oil, plus extra for drizzling
1 onion, sliced
1 leek, sliced
1 garlic clove, crushed
2 sprigs thyme, leaves picked
3 big handfuls spinach, chopped
1 tsp wholegrain mustard
60g cheddar, grated

Heat the oven to 200°C (180°C fan)/gas 6. Prick the potatoes all over and transfer to a baking tray. Drizzle with oil, sprinkle with salt and bake for about 1¼ hours, until tender. Meanwhile, heat the oil in a pan and cook the onion, leek, garlic, thyme and some seasoning for 15 minutes. Stir in the spinach until wilted, then remove from the heat. Once the potatoes are tender, remove from the oven and let cool a little. Halve them, scoop out the flesh and mash it. Mix the potato into the spinach mix with the mustard and most of the cheese (reserve a handful). Pile the mix back into the potato skins, sprinkle with the remaining cheese and return to the oven for 15 minutes. Serves 2.

Crab and spinach risotto

A risotto is the perfect foil for delicate crab and a vibrant blend of spinach and lemon.

800ml stock
60g spinach
2 tbsp pine nuts, toasted
Half a lemon, zested and juiced
Olive oil
Small bunch spring onions, finely sliced
1 garlic clove, crushed
150g arborio rice
100ml white wine
30g parmesan, grated
200g white crabmeat
Large handful parsley, chopped

Put the stock in a pan and bring to the boil. Blanch the spinach in the stock, then scoop out and let it cool a little. Squeeze out the liquid and transfer to a blender with the pine nuts, lemon juice, 2 tbsp olive oil and some salt and pepper. Blitz until smooth. Then heat a glug of oil in a large pan and fry the spring onions for 5 minutes, then stir in the garlic and continue cooking for a minute. Stir in the rice, coating in the oil, and cook for another minute. Pour in the wine, let it evaporate, then turn down the heat. Add the stock a ladleful at a time, letting each one absorb before adding the next and stirring often; this should take about 20 minutes. When the rice is cooked, stir through the blitzed spinach, parmesan, lemon zest, crab and parsley. Serves 2.

Spinach gnudi

1 tbsp olive oil
1 garlic clove, chopped
250g spinach
200g ricotta
40g parmesan, grated
Pinch of grated nutmeg
1 egg
1 lemon, zested
2 tbsp flour

You don't want to cook these fluffy Italian dumplings in rolling boiling water, you're looking for more of a shake. Serve them with melted butter and a sprinkling of parmesan.

Heat the oil in a pan, then cook the garlic for a minute. Add the spinach and cook until wilted, then leave to cool. Once cool enough to handle, squeeze out all the liquid, then chop and transfer to a bowl. Combine the spinach with the ricotta, parmesan, nutmeg, egg, lemon zest, flour and some seasoning. Shape into eight balls, then chill for 1 hour. Bring a pan of salted water to the boil, then cook the gnudi gently until they bob to the surface. Scoop out and serve. Makes 8.

Chicken with lemon and spinach

1 tbsp oil
4 skin-on, bone-in
  chicken thighs
2 shallots, sliced
1 garlic clove, chopped
100ml white wine
100ml stock
150g spinach
Half a lemon

A simple dish to eat as is or with steamed rice, potatoes or extra greens.

Heat the oil in a pan, then add the chicken, skin-side down, and cook gently until caramelized all over, about 30 minutes. Add the shallots and garlic, cook until softened, then tip in the wine and let it bubble away until evaporated. Pour in the stock, bring to a simmer, then stir through the spinach to wilt. Add a squeeze of lemon juice and some seasoning. Serves 2.

Baked spinach frittata

1 tbsp olive oil
1 onion, chopped
150g cherry tomatoes,
  halved
200g spinach
5 eggs
Half a lemon, zested
  and juiced
60g feta

A dollop or two of tomato chutney would make a fine accompaniment, whether for brunch or dinner.

Heat the oil in a frying pan then cook the onion until softened, about 10 minutes. Add the tomatoes, cook for 2 minutes, then add the spinach and cook until wilted. In a large bowl, beat the eggs, then stir in the spinach mix, lemon zest and juice, feta and some seasoning. Grease a baking dish, pour in the egg mix and bake at 200°C (180°C fan)/gas 6 for 25 minutes, or until set. Serves 4.

Carrot

I've always liked carrots but often do little more with them than dunk into dips, roast with honey or harissa, throw into dals, or combine with garlic, onion and celery for a sofrito to get soups, stews, sauces and rice dishes going. As they're with us all year round, they often get sidelined in favour of more seasonal stars — but it doesn't have to be this way. Carrots are not only wonderfully robust and versatile, but they're also incredibly forgiving in terms of cooking (eat raw, boiled, roasted or in a stir-fry), making them the ultimate kitchen companion.

SEASON	Late spring to early summer
PAIR WITH	Pork, feta, parmesan, beetroot, red onion, orange, maple syrup, harissa, yoghurt, paprika, cumin, cardamom, coriander, parsley, cashews, dates.
HACK	If you buy a bunch of carrots, don't ditch the carrot tops; use them to make pesto or chimichurri.

Paprika-roasted carrots with parsley dressing

500g carrots, halved
    (quartered if large)
Olive oil
1 tbsp paprika
1 tbsp cumin seeds, crushed
20g pistachios, chopped
20ml white wine vinegar
Drizzle of honey
50g parsley

These smoky-sweet carrots make a good side for roast chicken, or bulk them up with crisp chickpeas to turn them into lunch.

Put the carrots in a roasting tin, drizzle with oil and add the spices and some seasoning. Toss to coat, then roast at 200°C (180°C fan)/ gas 6 for 30 minutes until tender. Meanwhile, put the pistachios, vinegar, a big drizzle of honey, 2 tbsp olive oil, the parsley and some salt and pepper in a blender. Blitz until smooth, then taste and add more honey if you like. Transfer the carrots to a serving plate and spoon over the parsley dressing. Serves 4.

Carrot cake cheesecake

150g plain flour
1 tsp baking powder
½ tsp bicarbonate of soda
1 tsp cinnamon
1 tsp mixed spice
1 orange, zested, plus the
    juice of half
150g carrots, grated
60g pecans, chopped,
    plus extra to serve
2 eggs
120g light brown sugar
120ml light olive oil

FOR THE TOPPING
250g soft cheese
80g icing sugar
Half an orange, zested
1 tsp vanilla extract
½ tsp ground ginger
100ml double cream

Two become one in this carrot cake-cheesecake hybrid.

In a large bowl, combine the flour, baking powder, bicarb, spices, orange zest and a pinch of salt. Stir in the carrots and nuts. In a second bowl, whisk the eggs, sugar, oil and orange juice, then pour into the dry ingredients and combine. Tip into a lined 22cm round cake tin and bake at 180°C (160°C fan)/gas 4 for 35-40 minutes, until a skewer inserted into the middle comes out clean. Set aside to cool. To make the topping, beat the soft cheese, icing sugar, orange zest, vanilla and ginger until smooth. Pour in the cream and beat again. Spoon over the cooled cake and put in the fridge to chill for 3-4 hours. Serve scattered with more pecans, if you like. Serves 8-10.

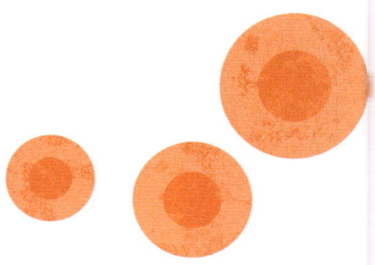

Carrot and coriander crepes

150g gram flour
1 tsp ground turmeric
1 tsp cumin seeds, crushed
2 tbsp olive oil, plus extra for frying
120g carrots, grated
Large handful coriander, leaves chopped
1 garlic clove, crushed

These are super easy, which means you can concentrate on having fun with the toppings: roasted beetroot and dill, perhaps, roasted tomatoes and a fried egg, or double down on the carrot theme with the paprika-roasted carrots opposite.

Put the flour, turmeric and cumin seeds in a large bowl, add the oil and 150ml water and whisk until you have a batter. Stir in the carrots, coriander and garlic, season to taste, then set the mix aside for 30 minutes. Heat a little oil in a non-stick frying pan, then spoon in a quarter of the batter, swirling around the pan. Cook for 1–2 minutes, until bubbles appear, then flip and cook on the other side for a minute. Transfer to a plate and repeat with the remaining batter. Makes 4.

Carrot and tahini soup

Olive oil
1 onion, diced
2 garlic cloves, finely chopped
400g carrots, finely chopped
½ tsp ground cumin
¼ tsp ground coriander
750ml stock
Half a lemon, juiced
2 tbsp tahini

If you have the time and inclination, add a nice bit of texture by roasting chickpeas in the oven until crisp to spoon over the finished soup.

Heat a good glug of oil in a heavy-based pan, then cook the onion until soft, about 10 minutes. Stir through the garlic, then add the carrots, cumin and coriander and cook until the carrots have softened. Tip in the stock, season with salt and pepper, then simmer, covered, for 15 minutes. Blitz with a hand blender until smooth, then stir through the lemon juice and tahini. Serves 4.

Carrot marmalade

300g carrots, grated
Thumb-sized piece of ginger, grated
2 tsp cumin seeds, ground
Half an orange, zested and juiced
1 lemon, zested and juiced
60g sugar

This is something to eat with cheese, on toast or a crumpet; alternatively, with crackers.

Put all the ingredients apart from the sugar in a large saucepan. Pour in 200ml water, bring to the boil, then reduce the heat and simmer for 30 minutes. Tip in the sugar and continue simmering for 15 minutes, then transfer to a sterilized jar. Makes about 400g.

Cucumber

Crisp, cool and refreshing – well, cucumbers do have a water content of 95 per cent. They are what you want on the hottest days, in chopped salads, Greek salads, or any other salad for that matter. Or try them pickled; with noodles; whizzed into soups, dips and sauces (with soy sauce, rice wine vinegar and peanut butter); or added to cocktails. Cucumbers are also an excellent foil for spicy food, combined with yoghurt and mint, for example, or cubed and added to curries.

SEASON	Early summer to mid-autumn
VARIETIES	Long cucumbers are perfect for soups, sandwiches and cocktails, while the smaller, crisper varieties hold their shape a little better, so use in salads.
HACK	If a recipe calls for scooping out the watery core, save and pop it into the blender to whizz up your next juice or peanutty sauce for noodles.

Smacked cucumber with feta and za'atar

1 cucumber
1 tbsp olive oil
1 garlic clove, sliced
1 tbsp za'atar
1 tbsp lime juice
50g feta

Smacking cucumber is a Chinese technique that allows the veg to soak up all the dressing.

Put the cucumber on a board and use a rolling pin to break it open. Tear the cucumber into pieces and transfer to a bowl with a pinch of salt; set aside for 10 minutes. Meanwhile, heat the oil in a small pan. Add the garlic, cook for 2 minutes, then add the za'atar and leave to cool. Stir in the lime juice. To serve, put the cucumber on a serving dish, spoon over the dressing and toss. Crumble over the feta. Serves 4 as a side.

Cucumber and lime cooler

Half a cucumber, chopped
3 limes, juiced
Handful mint leaves
1 tbsp caster sugar
Soda water, to serve

No soda water? Top with sparkling water instead.

Put all the ingredients apart from the soda water in a blender and blitz until smooth. Strain through a sieve into a jug. Put a large ice cube in each of four glasses and divide the cucumber mix between them. Top up with soda water. Makes 4.

Herby cucumber tartines

25g coriander
5g mint leaves
Half a green chilli,
  roughly chopped
1 small garlic clove,
  roughly chopped
Half a lemon
Olive oil
2 slices sourdough
Half a small (Lebanese)
  cucumber, finely sliced

The green sauce can easily be doubled if you have more mouths to feed.

Put the herbs, chilli and garlic in a food processor. Add a good squeeze of lemon juice, a drizzle of oil and a pinch of salt and blitz. Toast the bread, then slather with the green sauce. Top with cucumber slices. Serves 2.

Peanut and chicken banh mi

1 small cucumber,
  cut into batons
2 tsp rice wine vinegar
40g salted peanuts
50ml hoisin sauce
2 skinless and boneless
  chicken thighs
1 baguette
Mayonnaise
A few baby gem
  lettuce leaves
A few mint leaves
A few coriander leaves

Once these Vietnamese sandwiches are assembled, add a squeeze of sriracha, if you like.

In a bowl, toss the cucumber with the rice wine vinegar and set aside. Meanwhile, put the peanuts, hoisin sauce and 2 tsp water in a blender and blitz. Put the chicken in a bowl, tip over the sauce and set aside for 30 minutes. Transfer the lot to a baking tray and cook at 220°C (200°C fan)/gas 7 for 40 minutes, until cooked through. Cut the baguette in half, then split it lengthways. Spread the inside with mayonnaise then top with the lettuce. Slice the chicken, pat the cucumber dry, then stuff both inside the baguette halves with the herbs. Serves 2.

Chopped salad with chickpeas and sumac yoghurt

1 cucumber, chopped
10 cherry tomatoes,
  chopped
1 stick celery, chopped
5 radishes, chopped
200g jarred chickpeas,
  drained
Large handful coriander,
  leaves chopped

FOR THE DRESSING
150g yoghurt
2 tsp olive oil
Half a lemon, juiced
½ tsp sumac
1 small garlic clove, crushed

Some croutons wouldn't go amiss here, or leftover pitta toasted in the oven.

Put all the salad ingredients in a salad bowl and toss together. In a small bowl, combine all the dressing ingredients with a pinch of salt. Spoon over the chopped salad and mix well. Serves 4-6.

Pepper

Sweet, crisp and versatile, peppers are the laid-back friend in the group. Whether bell peppers or romano, you can, of course, use them raw in salads and wraps, but it's when they're cooked that their real sweet-and-sour personality comes to the fore. Slice and add to paellas or baked eggs, blister over a hot flame or barbecue to whizz with nuts into dips, or – and this is my favourite way of all – stuff them, with meat, pulses or veg for all the holiday vibes.

SEASON	Midsummer to early autumn
VARIETIES	The standard mild, sweet bell peppers, coming in red, yellow and green, add crunch to salads or stir-fries; the long, full-flavoured romano peppers, meanwhile - small, sweet and looking like chillies - are extra sweet, ideal for adding to salads or stuffing with cheese (ricotta or feta, say).
PAIR WITH	Feta, halloumi, eggs, anchovies, tomatoes, aubergines, potatoes, green beans, paprika, chilli, basil, thyme, pomegranate molasses, tahini.

Pepper and spiced rice boats

1 tbsp coconut oil,
plus extra for greasing
1 onion, finely chopped
2 garlic cloves, finely
chopped
1 green chilli, finely
chopped
½ tsp ground cumin
½ tsp ground coriander
½ tsp ground turmeric
200ml stock
2 tbsp coconut milk
80g basmati rice, rinsed
2 romano peppers, halved
and deseeded

Stuffed peppers have a lot going for them: they're easy to make, can be served warm or at room temperature and work with grilled fish, potatoes, salads or solo.

Heat the oil in a pan, then cook the onion until softened, about 10 minutes. Stir in the garlic, chilli and spices and cook for a minute. Pour in the stock and coconut milk, bring to the boil, then turn down the heat. Add the rice and cook, covered, until the rice is cooked and the liquid has been absorbed, about 15 minutes. Spoon the rice into the pepper halves, transfer to a lightly greased baking dish and bake at 200°C (180°C fan)/gas 6 for 25 minutes. Serves 2.

Pepper and paprika scramble

1 large onion,
finely chopped
2 red peppers,
finely chopped
2 garlic cloves,
finely chopped
2 tbsp olive oil,
plus extra for frying
1 tbsp tomato puree
1 tsp paprika
8 cherry tomatoes,
chopped
100g halloumi, cubed
4 eggs
Large handful parsley,
chopped
Toast, to serve

I first discovered scrambles at a market in San Francisco, where they were making them to order with seasonal vegetables. They've now become my weekend staple.

In a large frying pan, cook the onion, peppers and garlic in the oil for 10 minutes, until softened. Stir in the tomato puree followed by the paprika and tomatoes, then continue cooking for 10 minutes and season with salt and pepper. Meanwhile, heat a glug of oil in a non-stick frying pan and fry the halloumi cubes on each side until golden; transfer to a plate lined with kitchen paper. Back to the pepper pan: crack in the eggs and scramble over a low heat. When the eggs are cooked, stir through the parsley. Serve topped with the halloumi and with toast on the side. Serves 2.

Red pepper paella

500ml hot stock
Pinch of saffron
Olive oil
1 onion, finely chopped
2 garlic cloves, crushed
1 large tomato, chopped
2 red peppers, chopped
1 tsp paprika
150g paella rice
100ml wine
Half a lemon
Large handful parsley,
  chopped
Handful black olives,
  stoned and chopped

While paella rice is readily available, you could use arborio instead.

Combine the hot stock and saffron, then set aside. In a large frying pan, heat a good glug of oil, then add the onion, garlic and a pinch of salt and cook for 10 minutes. Stir in the tomato and peppers, cook for 5 minutes, then add the paprika. Tip in the rice and continue cooking, stirring, for a few minutes. Pour in the wine, let it bubble away, then pour in the stock. Bring it to the boil and cook, uncovered, over a low-medium heat for 20 minutes. Add a good squeeze of lemon juice, then scatter over the parsley and olives. Serves 2-3.

Pepper chow mein

2 nests of dried egg
  noodles
Sesame oil
2 garlic cloves, sliced
Large pinch of dried chilli
  flakes
2 red peppers, finely sliced
4 spring onions, sliced
  lengthways
1 tbsp soy sauce
1 tbsp rice wine vinegar
1 tsp honey

This is so quick to pull together. I've used red peppers, but this would be a good opportunity to use green peppers, too.

Cook the noodles in salted boiling water according to the packet instructions. Drain, rinse under cold water, then toss with a little sesame oil. Heat a wok, add 1 tbsp oil, then add the garlic and chilli and cook for 30 seconds. Add the peppers, continue cooking for 3 minutes, then add the noodles and the remaining ingredients and cook for a final 4 minutes. Drizzle with a little more sesame oil and divide between bowls. Serves 2.

Peperonata

2 tbsp olive oil
1 large red onion, sliced
3 garlic cloves, sliced
1 red chilli, chopped
2 red peppers, sliced
2 yellow peppers, sliced
400g tin plum tomatoes
½ tsp dried oregano
Good splash of red
  wine vinegar

Spoon this onto pasta with lashing of grated parmesan, or serve on the side of sausages.

Heat the oil in a large pan then cook the onion, garlic and chilli for 10 minutes. Add the peppers and a pinch of salt, cover and continue cooking for 15 minutes, stirring occasionally. Tip in the tomatoes, breaking them up with a spoon, then add the oregano and simmer for 30 minutes. Season and add a good splash of vinegar. Serves 2 as a main, 4 as a side.

Mushroom

The mushroom kingdom is a magical place. The varieties now available, from portobello to porcini, oyster to shiitake, are extensive and can pack a umami punch in so many meals, spanning the globe. Their meaty texture makes them a mainstay of plant-based cooking, but they also pair well with meat. While different mushrooms behave in wonderfully different ways, one commonality is their sponge-like quality, soaking up whatever flavours you choose to throw at them. They do, however, hold a lot of liquid, so when it comes to cooking it pays to be patient (and use a searing heat), because no one wants squishy mushrooms.

SEASON	Mid-autumn for wild mushrooms; otherwise all year round
PREP	Don't wash your mushrooms as they will absorb the water. Instead, brush or wipe them with a cloth.
PAIR WITH	Chicken, steak, parmesan, taleggio, chestnuts, butternut squash, kale, spinach, pak choi, leeks, sage, tarragon, miso, harissa, soy sauce.

Mushroom shawarma

150g oyster mushrooms, cut into strips

250g chestnut mushrooms, quartered

1 red onion, cut into wedges

1 tsp ground cumin

¾ tsp ground coriander

1 tsp smoked paprika

2 garlic cloves, finely chopped

50ml olive oil

1 preserved lemon, flesh discarded, rind chopped

A hands-off dish to eat stuffed inside pittas with chopped salad.

Put all the ingredients in a large bowl, add a good pinch of salt and combine well. Tip the lot into a baking tray and cook in the oven at 220°C (200°C fan)/gas 7 for 40 minutes, stirring halfway through. Serves 4.

Dirty rice with mushrooms

140g basmati rice

Oil

1 onion, finely chopped

2 garlic cloves, chopped

300g chestnut mushrooms, finely chopped

1 tbsp cajun seasoning

100ml stock

1 tbsp soy sauce

4 spring onions, sliced

Big handful parsley, leaves chopped

Mushrooms work particularly well in this fragrant African-American rice dish. It's worth noting that cajun seasoning varies in heat and saltiness, so taste and adjust as you see fit.

Cook the rice in a pan of salted boiling water according to packet instructions then drain and set aside. Heat a drizzle of oil in a frying pan, then add the onion and garlic and cook for 5 minutes. Add the mushrooms, cajun seasoning and some salt and continue cooking until the mushrooms have softened and the water has evaporated. Tip in the stock and soy sauce and continue cooking until the liquid has evaporated, about 5 minutes. Take off the heat, then stir through the cooked rice, spring onions and parsley. Serves 2-4.

Harissa mushrooms with butter bean hummus

4 portobello mushrooms

2 tbsp olive oil

Half a lemon, juiced, plus an extra squeeze for the hummus

2 tbsp rose harissa

Drizzle of honey

400g tin butter beans, drained

1 garlic clove, chopped

2 tbsp tahini

The mushrooms absorb all the sweet, smoky and spicy notes of the harissa, which is tempered by the silky-smooth butter beans.

In a bowl, combine the mushrooms, 1 tbsp olive oil, the lemon juice, harissa and a big drizzle of honey; put in the fridge for an hour. Meanwhile, make the hummus. Put the butter beans, garlic, tahini, 1 tbsp olive oil, a squeeze of lemon juice and 1 tbsp of water in a blender and blitz until smooth. Tip the mushrooms and marinade into a baking tray and roast at 180°C (160°C fan)/gas 4 for 30 minutes. Spoon the hummus onto a dish and top with the mushrooms and any leftover marinade. Serves 2-4.

Mushroom and radicchio ragu

Spoon this veg-laden ragu onto cooked rigatoni or polenta.

1 onion, roughly chopped
1 carrot, roughly chopped
1 stick celery, roughly chopped
2 tbsp olive oil
2 garlic cloves, crushed
Pinch of chilli flakes
1 tsp chopped rosemary leaves
1 bay leaf
100ml red wine
4 tbsp tomato puree
350g chestnut mushrooms
100ml stock
Half a radicchio, shredded

Pulse the onion, carrot and celery in a food processor until finely chopped. Heat the oil in a large pan and fry the vegetables until soft. Add the garlic, chilli flakes, rosemary and bay and cook for 2 minutes. Tip in the red wine, let it evaporate, then stir in the tomato puree. Blitz the mushrooms in the food processor, then tip into the pan along with the stock and cook for 20 minutes. Remove the bay leaf, season and stir through the radicchio. Serves 4.

Mushroom, leek and tarragon crumble

I use spelt flour in the crumble, but really you can use whatever you have to hand, whether that's plain or wholemeal.

2 tbsp olive oil
3 leeks, sliced
1 garlic clove, chopped
250g chestnut mushrooms, sliced
100ml stock
400g tin chopped tomatoes
Large handful parsley, chopped
100g spelt flour
100g oats
Handful tarragon, leaves chopped
40g butter
60g cheddar, grated
1 tsp wholegrain mustard

Heat the oil in an ovenproof pan, then cook the leeks, stirring occasionally, for 10 minutes, until soft. Stir in the garlic, cook for a minute, then add the mushrooms, stock, tomatoes, parsley and some seasoning and cook for 5 minutes more. Meanwhile, combine the flour, oats, tarragon and some seasoning in a large bowl. Rub in the butter, then stir in the cheese and mustard. Tip the crumble over the filling, then bake at 200°C (180°C fan)/gas 6 for 20 minutes, until bubbling. Serves 4.

Potato

Who doesn't love potatoes? Whether roasted, mashed, cut into chips or simply boiled and buttered, potatoes in their various guises are there ready, every day, all year round. There are hundreds of varieties to choose from, but it's important to get the right one for the job. King Edward and Maris Piper are good all-rounders and are destined to be roasted, mashed or turned into chips; Charlottes should be steamed or boiled and served simply with a bit of butter or used for potato salad (pink firs work a treat here, too). Come spring, Jersey royals, waxy on the inside and flimsy of skin on the outside, enter the arena with their distinctive sweet, nutty flavour – ideal for salads or sliced to top a pizza bianca. They really can do it all.

SEASON	All year round
PAIR WITH	Mussels, salmon, tuna, anchovies, pancetta, chicken, duck, dill, mint, rosemary, peas, leeks, courgettes, asparagus, mushrooms, cavolo nero, crème fraîche, cheese, apples, lemon, cornichons, mustard, paprika, turmeric, chaat masala, sauerkraut.
HACK	To quickly peel your spuds, run a sharp knife around the middle before boiling. Once cooked, the skin should come right off.

Kale Caesar on smashed parmesan potatoes

You could easily swap the kale for cavolo nero here.

500g new potatoes
3 tbsp olive oil
15g parmesan, grated, plus extra to serve
2 garlic cloves: 1 finely chopped, 1 crushed
4 tbsp tahini
1 lemon, juiced
2 tsp Dijon mustard
250g kale, stems discarded, leaves torn

Bring a pan of salted water to the boil, add the potatoes and cook for 15 minutes, or until cooked through; drain well. In a roasting tin, combine 2 tbsp olive oil with the parmesan, the finely chopped garlic and some seasoning. Add the potatoes, toss, then squash gently with the base of a glass. Bake at 190°C (170°C fan)/gas 5 for 40 minutes. Meanwhile, combine the tahini, lemon juice, remaining 1 tbsp oil, crushed garlic, mustard and some seasoning in a bowl. Whisk in 2 tbsp water and set aside. In a large bowl, massage the kale with a pinch of salt until the leaves have darkened and reduced, then toss with the dressing. To serve, spoon the potatoes into bowls, top with the kale and some more grated parmesan. Serves 2.

Mashed potato, kimchi and sweetcorn cakes

These are so easy to pull together and mainly from store cupboard ingredients to boot.

600g floury potatoes, quartered
100g kimchi, chopped
10g coriander leaves, chopped
100g tinned sweetcorn, drained
1 lime, zested
2 spring onions, sliced
2 tbsp plain flour
Oil, for frying

Boil the potatoes in a pan of salted water until tender, about 15 minutes. Drain well and leave to air-dry a little. Tip into a large bowl and mash. Mix in the remaining ingredients (except the oil) and season well, then shape into eight patties. Heat a little oil in a frying pan and, once hot, cook the patties on both sides until golden. Makes 8.

Salt and vinegar new potatoes

Salty, sticky and sweet, these spuds bring seaside holiday vibes.

500g new potatoes, halved
1 tbsp olive oil
1 sprig rosemary, leaves finely chopped
1 tbsp balsamic vinegar

In a roasting tin, toss the potatoes, oil, rosemary, ½ tsp salt and a generous grind of black pepper. Roast at 240°C (220°C fan)/gas 9 for 30 minutes, until golden and tender. Crush slightly with the bottom of a glass, then drizzle over the balsamic vinegar. Return to the oven for 10 minutes until crisp. Serves 4.

Potato and red pepper quesadillas

Quesadillas are a great simple supper - just add spoonfuls of tomato salsa and/or guacamole.

350g potatoes, cut into chunks
1 tbsp oil
5 spring onions, sliced
1 small red chilli, chopped
½ tsp paprika
50g jarred roasted red peppers, chopped
50g manchego, grated
Half a lime
Large handful parsley, chopped, stems and all
2 soft tortillas

Cook the potatoes in a pan of salted boiling water until cooked through, about 15 minutes; drain and leave to cool. Meanwhile, heat the oil in a frying pan, then add the spring onions, chilli and paprika and cook, stirring, until softened. Tip the potatoes into a large bowl and mash. Stir in the spring onion mix, peppers, cheese, a squeeze of lime juice and the parsley. Season. Take a tortilla, spoon half the filling over one half, then fold over. Repeat with the second tortilla. In the same frying pan, toast the quesadillas for a few minutes on each side. Serves 2.

Potato pav bhaji

Spread this on hot buttered bread rolls for one of the best lunches around.

300g potatoes, cut into chunks
100g frozen peas
1 tbsp oil
Knob of butter
1 red onion, chopped
1 red chilli, chopped
3 garlic cloves, finely chopped
Thumb-sized piece of ginger, finely chopped
½ tsp ground turmeric
1 tsp coriander seeds, toasted and ground
1 tsp cumin seeds, toasted and ground
6 vine tomatoes (about 80g), chopped
Half a red pepper, chopped
Half a lemon, zested and juiced
1 large carrot, cut into small dice
1 tsp garam masala
Large handful coriander, chopped

Cook the potatoes in salted boiling water until soft, adding the peas in the last few minutes; drain then mash roughly. Heat the oil and butter in a heavy-based pan, then fry the onion and chilli until soft. Add the garlic, ginger, turmeric, coriander and cumin seeds, cook for 2 minutes, then tip in the tomatoes, red pepper and lemon zest and continue cooking for 5 minutes. Stir in the carrot, garam masala, potato mixture, a pinch of salt and 100ml water. Continue cooking for 10 minutes, adding more liquid if it starts to stick. Remove from the heat, and stir through the lemon juice and coriander. Serves 4.

Kale

Kale is the modern-day spinach, containing more vitamin C than its predecessor, as well as the likes of calcium and vitamins E and K. That's not to say this variety of cabbage isn't tasty; it often requires little more than olive oil and garlic to showcase its talents. Kale ranges from the curly kind to straight-leaved Italian cavolo nero, but the common thread is its robust and fibrous nature, meaning it lasts well in the fridge. What is particularly pleasing about this leafy green, though, is it can turn its hand to most things: eat raw in salads, massaging the leaves with oil and salt; blitz into smoothies; crisp up in the oven; or treat it with longer cooking times in stews, sauces and soup, where kale's slight bitterness will mellow.

SEASON	Early autumn to mid-spring
PREP	Strip the leaves from the tough central stems using a knife (or your hands), then chop or shred.
HACK	When roasted, kale takes on a deeply savoury personality and crisps up nicely, which is ideal for adding texture to dishes or simply snacking on. Toss 200g kale leaves with 2 tbsp oil and a pinch of salt, then spread out on a baking tray. Roast at 200°C (180°C fan)/gas 6 for 8–10 minutes, turning halfway through.

Ribollita meets cassoulet

Olive oil
1 red onion, chopped
2 garlic cloves, chopped
1 red chilli, chopped
1 large carrot, chopped
3 sticks celery, chopped
2 sprigs rosemary, leaves
  roughly chopped
400g tin chopped
  tomatoes
570g jar white beans,
  drained
100g cavolo nero, stems
  discarded, leaves torn
400ml stock
3 slices sourdough,
  roughly torn
30g parmesan, grated

When the classic Italian soup fraternizes with a French cassoulet. Rather than stirring in the bread, it's torn and drizzled with oil for an almost crouton-like topping.

Heat a good glug of oil in an ovenproof saucepan or casserole on the hob. Add the onion, garlic, chilli, carrot, celery and some salt and pepper and cook for 10 minutes until softened. Stir in the rosemary, cook for a minute, then tip in the tinned tomatoes, beans, cavolo nero and stock. Give it a stir and simmer for 5 minutes until the leaves have wilted. Nestle the torn bread into the bean mix, drizzle with oil, then scatter over the parmesan. Put in the oven at 200°C (180°C fan)/gas 6 for 30 minutes. Serves 4.

Kale and ricotta dumplings

150g kale, stems discarded,
  leaves roughly torn
250g ricotta
25g parmesan, grated
10g dill, finely chopped
Half a lemon, zested
  and juiced
1 egg
3 tbsp plain flour

These neat balls are best served on a bed of tomato sauce, with a grating of nutmeg.

Blanch the kale in boiling water for a few minutes, then drain and leave to cool. Squeeze out as much water as you can, then finely chop the leaves. In a large bowl, add the cheeses, kale, dill, lemon zest and juice, egg, flour and season with salt and a generous grind of black pepper. Stir to combine, then roll spoonfuls of the mixture into small balls (about 12). Put in the fridge for 30 minutes. Cook the dumplings in salted boiling water for 4 minutes, then spoon into bowls. Serves 2-4, depending on hunger.

Kale and hazelnut pesto

100g kale, stems discarded,
  leaves torn
50g toasted hazelnuts
1 garlic clove, peeled
50ml olive oil
30g parmesan, grated
Half a lemon, juiced

If this is destined for pasta, scoop out the kale once cooked and use the same water to boil your chosen pasta shape.

Blanch the kale for 1 minute in salted boiling water, then drain and cool a little. Squeeze out as much water as possible. In a food processor, blitz the nuts and garlic, then add the kale and blitz again. With the motor still running, add the olive oil and finally the parmesan and a good squeeze of lemon juice. Taste and add more lemon juice, if needed. Serves 2-3.

Crispy kale, peanut and lime noodles

The world loves a peanut sauce and it's not hard to see why. Here, it makes the ideal partner for crisp kale and slippery noodles.

200g kale, stems discarded, leaves roughly torn
3 tbsp sesame oil
100g peanut butter
2 tbsp tahini
1 tbsp soy sauce
2 tsp honey
Thumb-sized piece of ginger, grated
1 small garlic clove, grated
1 lime, juiced
Pinch of chilli flakes
200g dried soba noodles
Lime wedges, to serve

Put the kale leaves on a baking tray, toss with 2 tbsp sesame oil and a good pinch of salt. Spread in a single layer, then roast at 200°C (180°C fan)/gas 6 for 8–10 minutes, turning halfway through, until crisp. Meanwhile, mix the peanut butter, tahini, soy sauce, honey, ginger, garlic, lime juice, chilli and the remaining 1 tbsp oil. Cook the noodles according to the packet instructions, then drain and rinse briefly under cold water. Combine noodles and sauce, then mix in the kale. Divide between bowls and serve with lime wedges. Serves 2.

Turmeric kale frittata with quick pickled onions

You can swap kale for cavolo nero, but don't forget the pickled onions because they really perk things up.

1 red onion, very finely sliced
1 lemon, juiced
1 tsp honey
1 tbsp oil
1 green chilli, finely chopped
100g kale, stems discarded, leaves chopped
½ tsp ground turmeric
6 eggs
1 large handful coriander, chopped

In a small bowl, combine the onion, lemon juice, honey and a pinch of salt; set aside. Heat the oil in a non-stick ovenproof frying pan over a medium heat. Add the chilli, cook for a minute, then add the kale, 1 tbsp water and the turmeric and cook until the kale has wilted. Meanwhile, crack the eggs into a large bowl, add a generous pinch of salt and a good grating of black pepper and the coriander and whisk with a fork. When the kale is ready, add that too. Tip the eggs into the frying pan and cook undisturbed for 5 minutes, until the eggs are nearly set. Transfer to the oven at 190°C (170°C fan)/ gas 5 and cook until set, about 8 minutes. Cut the frittata in half and serve with the pickled onions on top. Serves 2.

Asparagus

Perhaps spring's most iconic star, asparagus can be taken in many directions, from grilling to barbecuing, steaming to roasting. The first bunch, however, is best enjoyed as simply as possible, snapping off the woody ends, simmering until just tender and eaten with a bit of butter, or better yet, hollandaise. As the season progresses, that's the time to incorporate it into quiches, soups and anchovy pastas, or wrap spears in pancetta to dip in boiled eggs. The thing to remember, though, is that this delicate veg really is at its best when eaten fresh, so buy as close to home as possible. And it is pricey, so be sure to make use of the entire spear; tough ends can be finely sliced and added to stir-fries (cook with the alliums to ensure they soften).

SEASON	Mid-spring to early summer
PAIR WITH	Chicken, pancetta, chorizo, salmon (or hot-smoked salmon), crab, goat's cheese, taleggio, tomatoes, new potatoes, peas, broad beans, wild garlic, lemon, mustard, dill, pumpkin seeds, peanuts.
HACK	Asparagus and hollandaise is an unrivalled partnership, but you can really up the ante by adding brown butter (achieved by heating butter until the water evaporates and the milk solids caramelize) to your egg yolks when making the sauce.

Baked gnocchi with asparagus and pistachio pesto

450g gnocchi
200g asparagus, cut into 3cm pieces
1 leek, finely sliced
2 garlic cloves: 1 chopped, 1 crushed
Pinch of chilli flakes
1 lemon, zested, plus the juice of half
70ml olive oil
100g pistachios
15g basil
30g parmesan, grated

Gnocchi baked until crisp is the ultimate emergency dinner and can be on the table within half an hour.

Put the gnocchi in a large bowl, pour over boiling water to cover and leave to stand for 2 minutes, then drain well. Tip into a roasting tin with the asparagus, leek, the chopped garlic, a pinch of chilli, the lemon zest and some salt and pepper. Toss with 1½ tbsp of the olive oil, then put in the oven at 220°C (200°C fan)/gas 7 for 25 minutes. Meanwhile, put the remaining ingredients in a food processor with some salt and pepper and blend until you have a pesto consistency. Spoon half the pesto over the gnocchi, combine, then return to the oven for 5 minutes. Serve with the remaining pesto. Serves 2.

Asparagus panzanella with feta and mint

150g stale crusty bread, torn into pieces
3 tbsp olive oil
1 small red onion, finely sliced
250g asparagus, cut on the diagonal into 2cm pieces
Half a lemon, juiced
75g feta, crumbled
Large handful mint leaves, torn

There's no denying the allure of a traditional panzanella, but the formula for this Italian bread salad is worth exploring further. Subbing in asparagus, feta and mint is a good starting point.

Massage the bread with 1 tbsp oil, then spread out on a baking tray and put in a low oven until the bread is golden. Meanwhile, put the onion in a small bowl with a pinch of salt and set aside. Blanch the asparagus in a pan of salted boiling water for 3 minutes, then drain and leave to cool. In a large bowl, whisk the remaining 2 tbsp oil with the lemon juice and a pinch of salt. Add the asparagus, croutons and onion and toss well; set aside for 10 minutes. Stir in the feta and mint and season with black pepper. Serves 4.

Asparagus egg-fried rice

2 eggs
Sesame oil
Large thumb-sized piece of ginger, finely chopped
2 garlic cloves, finely chopped
130g long-grain rice, cooked and chilled
150g asparagus, cut into 2cm pieces
60g peas (fresh or frozen)
2 tbsp soy sauce
Bunch spring onions, sliced
Crispy chilli oil, to serve

This hinges on the rice being cold, so it's best to put it in the fridge overnight before making this dish.

Beat the eggs in a bowl and season. Heat a little oil in a frying pan, then tip in the eggs and scramble until set; set aside. Return the pan to the heat, add a little more oil and cook the ginger and garlic until fragrant, 1-2 minutes. Tip in the rice, breaking it up with a spoon, then add the asparagus, peas and soy sauce and keep cooking and stirring until the veg is cooked, about 5 minutes. Return the egg to the pan, cook for another 2 minutes, then stir through the spring onions. Serve drizzled with the crispy chilli oil. Serves 2.

Asparagus and gribiche toasts with garlic crumbs

Adding breadcrumbs here may feel like gilding the lily, but double carbs are always worth it.

2 eggs
1½ tbsp mayonnaise
1 tsp Dijon mustard
Big handful tarragon, chopped
Big handful parsley, chopped
1 tbsp chopped cornichons
120g asparagus
Olive oil
1 garlic clove, finely chopped
20g dried breadcrumbs
Half a lemon, zested
Toast, to serve

Boil the eggs for 8 minutes, then drain and cool under running water. Once cool enough to handle, peel then grate into a bowl. Add the mayo, mustard, herbs and cornichons and combine; set aside. Toss the asparagus spears in a little oil, then grill in a griddle pan until tender and charred, about 4 minutes. Add a drizzle of oil to another pan, then add the garlic and stir for a minute. Tip in the breadcrumbs and fry until golden, about 5 minutes; stir through the lemon zest. To serve, put the toast on two plates and top with the egg mix, followed by the asparagus and garlicky crumbs. Serves 2.

Asparagus and radish soba salad

You need a good amount of crunchy veg here, but do substitute any raw veg you have, such as cabbage or fennel.

200g asparagus
200g soba noodles
2 tbsp sesame oil
1 tbsp rice wine vinegar
3 tbsp soy sauce
1 tbsp honey
Thumb-sized piece of ginger, grated
1 small garlic clove, grated
Half a lime, juiced
1 carrot, julienned
100g radishes, finely sliced
100g cucumber, cut into half moons
Toasted sesame seeds, to serve
Coriander leaves, to serve

Blanch the asparagus in salted boiling water for 3 minutes, then drain and refresh under cold water; set aside. Once cool enough to handle, cut each stem into 3cm lengths. Cook the noodles according to packet instructions, then drain and refresh under cold water. In a large bowl, combine the sesame oil, vinegar, soy sauce, honey, ginger, garlic and lime juice. Add the noodles and veg and toss well. Serve topped with the sesame seeds and coriander leaves. Serves 2–3.

Brussels sprouts

Your relationship with this brassica most likely comes down to how you were first introduced (and specifically how long your family boiled them on 25th December). Sprouts aren't just for Christmas, mind. Given they act like little cabbages, there are myriad ways to show them off: roast, stir-fry, shave and serve raw in salads, or ferment and make into kimchi to stuff inside toasties. The world of sprouts opens up even further with the help of punchy harissa and gochujang, salty anchovies or soy sauce, and creamy, cheesy things. And don't disregard sprout tops (the leaves at the top of the stem) because they are a joy. Treat them like cabbage leaves, perhaps roasting with pomegranate molasses.

SEASON	Mid-autumn to early spring
PREP	Remove the outer leaves and trim the tip of the stalk. Toss with oil and roast for 30 minutes until golden or grill for about 4 minutes until charred and cooked through; shred or finely cut and use (raw) in salads. If boiling is your thing, you're looking at about 3 minutes for small to medium sprouts.
HACK	There's no such thing as too much pesto. For a riff on the green sauce, add halved sprouts and blend with the usual suspects (basil, garlic, parmesan, pine nuts, olive oil), plus a pinch of chilli.

Sprout and lemon casarecce

200g casarecce
2 tbsp olive oil, plus extra to serve
1 shallot, finely sliced
2 garlic cloves, sliced
220g Brussels sprouts, finely sliced
1 lemon, zested, plus 3 tbsp juice
50g grated parmesan
Pinch of chilli flakes
Handful toasted pine nuts, to serve

On an exceptionally cold night in Cambridge, Massachusetts, we took refuge with bowlfuls of pasta with lemony sprouts and lashings of parmesan at a restaurant called Pammy's. This is my version; I love it with casarecce (the short twists), but rigatoni or conchiglie are good alternatives.

Cook the pasta in salted boiling water according to the packet instructions, then drain, reserving some of the cooking water. Meanwhile, heat the oil in a heavy-based pan, then add the shallot, garlic and sprouts and cook for 7 minutes, stirring occasionally. Season generously with black pepper and a little salt, then stir in the lemon zest and continue cooking for 1 minute. Stir in the lemon juice and a good splash of the pasta cooking water, then add the cooked pasta, parmesan and a good pinch of chilli flakes. Toss everything together, adding more pasta water to loosen, if needed. Serve drizzled with olive oil and sprinkled with the pine nuts. Serves 2.

Sprout and comté tart

320g sheet puff pastry
2 tbsp natural yoghurt
1 tsp Dijon mustard
2 eggs
1 tbsp milk
1 garlic clove, crushed
100g comté, grated
1 tsp dried thyme
500g Brussels sprouts, shredded
40g walnuts, roughly broken

An easy, comforting puff pastry tart which is best served with a bitter leaf salad dressed with lemon juice and olive oil.

Unroll the pastry on a lined baking tray, score a 3cm border and prick the middle with a fork. Bake at 200°C (180°C fan)/gas 6 for 10 minutes, until golden. Meanwhile, in a large bowl, combine the yoghurt, mustard, eggs, milk, garlic, cheese, thyme and some seasoning. Remove the pastry from the oven and push down the middle with the back of a spoon. Spread half the yoghurt mix over the pastry, top with the shredded sprouts, then tip over the remaining yoghurt mix. Top with the walnuts and return to the oven for 15-20 minutes, until puffed up and golden. Serves 4-6.

Chipotle sprout tacos

500g Brussels sprouts, halved
2 garlic cloves, crushed
1 tbsp chipotle paste
1 tsp coriander seeds, crushed
1 tsp cumin seeds, crushed
Drizzle of olive oil
1 red onion, finely sliced
2 limes, juiced
Pinch of dried oregano
Corn tacos, to serve
Feta, crumbled, to serve
Coriander leaves, to serve

The punchy chipotle sprouts are balanced by creamy feta and zippy quick-pickled red onions.

On a baking tray, combine the first six ingredients then roast at 220°C (200°C fan)/gas 7 for 20 minutes. Meanwhile, in a small bowl, scrunch together the onion and a good pinch of salt; set aside for 15 minutes. Stir in the lime juice and oregano. Heat the tacos, then eat filled with spoonfuls of sprouts topped with the red onion, crumbled feta and a few coriander leaves. Serves 2-3.

Sprout gratin with sage pangrattato

3 tbsp olive oil
2 onions, halved and thickly sliced
600g Brussels sprouts, halved
80g chestnuts, chopped
50ml white wine
100ml stock
150ml double cream
100g dried breadcrumbs
15 sage leaves, chopped

Sprouts are yet more proof that potatoes don't have a monopoly on gratins. Feel free to mix up the pangrattato according to what you have, adding parmesan or roughly chopped walnuts, say.

Heat 2 tbsp oil in a large ovenproof pan. Add the onions and a pinch of salt and cook until soft, about 5 minutes. Add the sprouts, cook for 3 minutes, then add the chestnuts. Stir in the wine, stock and cream, then season with a good grind of black pepper. In a small bowl, combine the breadcrumbs, sage leaves and remaining 1 tbsp oil. Sprinkle the breadcrumbs over the sprouts, then transfer the dish to the oven at 220°C (200°C fan)/gas 7 and bake for 20 minutes until golden. Serves 4-6 as a side.

Sprout and caraway kraut

500g Brussels sprouts, finely sliced
2 carrots (about 100g), grated
1 heaped tsp caraway seeds
1 heaped tbsp sea salt flakes
½ tsp grated ginger

It's important to pack the kraut tightly inside the jar to keep as much air out as possible. The veg should be submerged in liquid; if the sprouts don't release enough, top up with filtered water.

Add all the ingredients to a large mixing bowl and set aside for 30 minutes. Massage everything together with your hands until liquid is released. Transfer the veg to a sterilized jar, packing it down as you go. Pour over the liquid from the bowl, making sure everything is fully submerged. Seal and leave at room temperature for 4 days. You want the veg to remain covered with liquid - if that's not the case, sprinkle with a little salt and top with filtered water. Once open, keep in the fridge for up to 2 months.

Chilli pepper

There are hundreds of varieties of chilli, grown everywhere from Mexico to India to Thailand to Spain, all performing different roles. And they're not just about heat; chillies bring sweet, sour, fruity, earthy and smoky notes, too. For me, they make up the holy trinity, alongside garlic and ginger, with serrano for stir-fries, bird's-eye for chopped salads, and jalapenos for guacamole being my most reached-for. It's worth remembering that size is also a factor: the smaller the chilli, the spicier it tends to be – after all, bird's-eye and scotch bonnet are among the hottest around. Once dried, though, a chilli's flavour intensifies; ancho, chipotle and pasilla work particularly well in rubs, pastes and sauces. That said, chilli flakes are always on hand for sauces – but err on the side of caution until you get to know their heat level.

SEASON	Early summer to mid-autumn
PAIR WITH	Chicken, prawns, crab, tofu, butternut squash, sweetcorn, avocado, hispi cabbage, black beans, miso, halloumi, mango, pineapple, lime, chocolate, tequila.
HACK	To get the most punch from a bird's-eye chilli (but without overwhelming a dish), cut a slit in the centre before adding it whole.

Chilli and tomato prawns

1 tbsp oil
1 shallot, finely chopped
2 garlic cloves,
 finely chopped
1 red chilli, finely chopped
400g tin chopped
 tomatoes
200g raw prawns
Large handful parsley,
 chopped

It's good sense to keep a bag of deveined prawns in the freezer, for a quick dinner such as this. Just add long pasta shapes, such as pappardelle.

Heat the oil in a frying pan, then add the shallot and cook for 4 minutes. Stir in the garlic and chilli, cook for 2 minutes, then tip in the tinned tomatoes and simmer for 15 minutes, until thickened and saucy. Add the prawns and cook over a high heat until they turn pink and are cooked through, about 10 minutes. Season and stir through the parsley. Serves 2.

Lime and chilli granita

100g caster sugar
5 limes, zest pared
 and juiced
1 red chilli, chopped

This is what you want on a hot summer night. To up the ante, serve in small glasses with a shot of tequila poured over the top.

Put the sugar, lime zest, chilli and 150ml water in a saucepan over a low heat. When it comes to a simmer and the sugar has dissolved, remove from the heat and set aside to cool. Squeeze in the lime juice and strain into a freezerproof container. Cover and freeze for 2 hours. Scrape the ice from the sides to break it up, then return to the freezer. Repeat this process every half an hour until frozen. Serves 4.

Chilli, crab and avocado crumpets

1 avocado
Half a lime, zested
 and juiced
200g white crabmeat
1 red chilli, finely chopped
1 tbsp mayonnaise
Handful coriander,
 leaves chopped
4 crumpets

This is a perfect lunch or light dinner, but you could also serve the crab mix on toast for an easy canape.

Peel and stone the avocado, then transfer the flesh to a bowl and mash with the lime zest and juice. Mix in the crab, chilli, mayonnaise, coriander and some seasoning. Toast the crumpets, then divide the mix equally between the crumpets. Serves 2.

Chilli oil

80ml neutral oil
4 garlic cloves, chopped
5 bird's-eye chillies, finely chopped
1 tbsp sesame oil
2 star anise
1 cinnamon stick
1 tbsp tomato paste

Pair this with starchy vegetables or eggs, or spoon onto noodles. This will keep in an airtight container in the fridge for 3 weeks.

Put the neutral oil in a pan over a low heat, then add the garlic and chillies and cook for 5 minutes, stirring often. Add the remaining ingredients and cook over a low heat for 15 minutes. Transfer to an airtight container.

No-bake chilli chocolate bars

100g butter
1 tbsp honey
200g digestive biscuits, crushed
30g roasted hazelnuts, chopped
150ml double cream
1 dried ancho chilli, stem removed, broken into pieces
200g dark chocolate, roughly broken

Mix things up by adding a bit of tequila to the melted chocolate, or vanilla if you prefer.

Melt the butter and honey in a pan. Put the crushed biscuits and hazelnuts in a bowl, pour over the melted butter and mix to combine. Add a pinch of salt, then tip into a lined 22cm square baking tin, pressing the mix into the base; transfer to the fridge. Heat the cream until steaming, then add the chilli and set aside for 1 hour. Bring the mix back to the boil, then strain through a sieve over the chocolate pieces in a bowl. Leave for a minute, then mix to melt. Pour the chocolate over the biscuit base, let it settle for 5 minutes, then transfer to the fridge until fully set. Slice into squares. Makes 10.

Swede

Not all vegetables are loved equally, and the humble swede is often cast aside, considered, well, just a bit boring. There is, however, much more to this pale veg than its appearance might suggest. Swede roasts well, it mashes well, it mingles well with other roots in mash-topped or pastry-lidded pies (its most famous appearance is, of course, in a Cornish pasty). However, it does need a helping hand, often in the form of spice (nutmeg, garam masala, turmeric), or fresh herbs (dill, rosemary, parsley, sage).

SEASON	Mid-autumn to late winter
PAIR WITH	Beef, chicken, sausages, carrots, parsnips, kale, apples, feta, parmesan, garam masala, turmeric, cumin, sage, maple syrup, gochujang, coconut milk.
HACK	For the easiest mash, pop a swede (skin and all) in a microwave for 20 minutes, then scoop out the flesh and mash. Job done.

Maple sausages, swede and apples

A warming one-pan dish to serve with a side of greens.

300g swede,
 cut into chunks
1 red onion, thinly sliced
1 tbsp olive oil
2 tbsp maple syrup
1 tbsp cider vinegar
6 sprigs thyme,
 leaves picked
6 sausages
2 apples, cut into chunks

Heat the oven to 200°C (180°C fan)/gas 6. Put the swede and red onion in a roasting tin and season well. In a small bowl, combine the oil, maple syrup, vinegar and thyme, then tip over the veg and toss well. Roast for 15 minutes, then add the sausages and apples, toss again to coat, and return to the oven for an hour. Serves 2.

Swede and bean carbonara with rocket

I'm a big fan of subbing in beans where you'd expect pasta. The creamy beans are the perfect foil for carbonara, pepped up with a handful of rocket.

1 tbsp olive oil
70g pancetta, diced
200g swede, cut into
 small chunks
1 large garlic clove,
 chopped
325g jar white beans
2 egg yolks
50g parmesan, grated
2 handfuls rocket, to serve

Heat the oil in a frying pan, then cook the pancetta until crispy, about 6 minutes; transfer to a plate lined with kitchen paper. Return the pan to the heat, then add the swede and cook until golden brown. Add the garlic, cook for a minute, then tip in the beans and their liquid and bring to the boil. Meanwhile, beat the egg yolks and parmesan, then season with a good grind of black pepper. When the swede is tender, remove the frying pan from the heat, tip in the egg mix and cooked pancetta and combine. Taste and check the seasoning, then serve with rocket on the side. Serves 2, generously.

Swede, carrot and mustard mash

Get ahead and make this the day before. When you're ready to serve, just reheat in a pan with a bit of butter.

1 large swede,
 cut into chunks
400g carrots,
 cut into chunks
1 garlic clove, peeled
1 tbsp wholegrain mustard

Bring a large pan of salted water to the boil, then add the swede, carrots and garlic clove and simmer for 30 minutes. Drain well, then mash with the mustard and some seasoning. Serves 4-6.

Parmesan and rosemary swede wedges

1 swede, cut into wedges
1 garlic clove, chopped
1 tsp chopped rosemary
1 tbsp olive oil
20g parmesan, grated

These moreish wedges go particularly well with fish such as haddock, or steak, in place of chips.

Heat the oven to 220°C (200°C fan)/gas 7. Put the swede wedges, garlic, chopped rosemary and olive oil on a baking tray. Season and toss well to coat. Roast for 20 minutes, turning halfway through, then sprinkle over the parmesan, toss again, and return to the oven for 10 minutes. Serves 4.

Swede and harissa shepherd's pie

Oil
1 onion, diced
2 carrots, diced
250g lamb mince
2 garlic cloves, crushed
1 tsp ground cumin
1 tbsp tomato puree
2 tbsp rose harissa
200ml stock
2 swedes, chopped
1 sweet potato, chopped
Large knob of butter

Here, the velvety smooth swede and sweet potato mash and gently spiced mince up the comfort ante.

Heat a good glug of oil in a heavy-based pan. Add the onion and carrots and cook until softened – about 10 minutes. Add the mince, breaking it up with the back of a spoon, and fry until crisp, about 5 minutes. Stir in the garlic, cumin, tomato puree, harissa and a pinch of salt. Cook for a few minutes, then tip in the stock and simmer, covered, for 30 minutes; tip into an ovenproof dish. Meanwhile, put the swede in a pan of cold salted water. Bring to the boil and cook for 10 minutes, then add the sweet potato and continue cooking for 15 minutes, until both are tender. Drain then mash with the butter and season. Spoon the mash on top of the filling, scuffing it with a fork. Bake at 190°C (170°C fan)/gas 5 for 40 minutes, until bubbling. Serves 2-3.

Pak choi

This leafy green Chinese cabbage (sometimes known as bok choy) is a weeknight workhorse; steam or stir-fry over a high heat and watch the leaves collapse while the white stems remain wonderfully crisp yet tender. Pak choi is my essential for any stir-fry, most noodle dishes (particularly ramen), and an unrivalled bed to lay salmon fillets or cubes of tofu on. It is, however, always better in the company of copious amounts of chilli, garlic, ginger and other bold flavours (think miso, sriracha).

SEASON	Late spring to late summer
PAIR WITH	Salmon, sea bass, prawns, beef, duck, tofu, sweetcorn, shiitake mushrooms, plums, sesame, lemongrass, ginger, miso, sriracha, five spice, cashews.
HEALTH	A good source of vitamins C and K, as well as folate and fibre.

Pak choi noodles with chilli oil eggs

Use whichever noodles you fancy: ramen, egg, udon – they all go well.

200g dried noodles
Sesame oil
1 shallot, chopped
1 garlic clove, chopped
Thumb-sized piece of
    ginger, chopped
2 pak choi, leaves separated
1 tbsp soy sauce
3 tsp chilli oil
2 eggs
Toasted sesame seeds,
    to serve

Cook the noodles according to packet instructions. Add a glug of oil to a large pan, then add the shallot, garlic and ginger, and cook until softened. Add the pak choi with a splash of water, cook for 2 minutes, then cover and continue cooking for another minute. Add the soy sauce, 2 tsp chilli oil and cooked noodles, and toss well; divide between two bowls. Heat the remaining chilli oil in a frying pan and, once sizzling, crack in the eggs and fry, occasionally spooning over the oil, until crispy around the edges. Slide the eggs on top of the noodles and scatter with sesame seeds. Serves 2.

Shiitake and pak choi stir-fry

This simple yet flavourful stir-fry is best served spooned over jasmine rice.

1 tbsp oil
2 shallots, finely chopped
2 garlic cloves,
    finely chopped
1 red chilli, chopped
1 lemongrass stalk, outer
    leaves discarded, core
    finely chopped
150g tomatoes, chopped
150g shiitake mushrooms,
    halved
1 tbsp kecap manis
3 pak choi, shredded

Heat the oil in a wok, then add the shallots and cook for 5 minutes. Add the garlic, chilli and lemongrass, and continue cooking for a couple of minutes. Stir in the tomatoes, cook for 10 minutes, then add the mushrooms and cook for another 4 minutes. Stir in the kecap manis and pak choi and continue cooking until the pak choi has wilted. Serves 2.

Roast pak choi with soy and ginger

The oven does the heavy lifting here. Eat with everything from meat to fish to tofu.

4 pak choi, leaves
    separated
Bunch spring onions,
    cut into 1cm lengths
1 garlic clove, crushed
1 red chilli, sliced
Thumb-sized piece of
    ginger, chopped
2 tbsp soy sauce
2 tsp sesame oil
1 lime, juiced

Combine all the ingredients in a roasting tin, then roast for 10 minutes at 180°C (160°C fan)/gas 4. Job done. Serves 2-4.

Leftover roast chicken noodle soup

A restorative home for any leftover roast chicken.

800ml stock
2 garlic cloves, chopped
Thumb-sized piece of ginger, grated
1 red chilli, sliced
2 nests of dried rice noodles
2 pak choi, leaves separated
200g leftover roast chicken, at room temperature, shredded
Half a lime, juiced
1 tsp soy sauce
2 spring onions, sliced
Handful Thai basil, chopped
Handful coriander, chopped
Lime wedges, to serve

Pour the stock into a large pan, then add the garlic, ginger and chilli, and bring to a simmer. Meanwhile, cook the noodles according to the packet instructions. Drain and rinse under cold water, then divide between two bowls. Drop the pak choi into the stock, simmer for 4 minutes, then add the chicken and continue cooking until it has heated through. Stir in the lime juice and soy sauce, then ladle over the noodles. Scatter over the spring onions and herbs and serve with wedges of lime. Serves 2.

Fish, pak choi and lemongrass parcels

You can mix up the veg here - try thinly sliced red pepper, or baby corn.

2 white fish fillets, such as halibut
Thumb-sized piece of ginger, grated
Half a lemongrass stalk, outer leaves discarded, core finely chopped
1 small red chilli, chopped
2 spring onions, sliced
2 pak choi, leaves separated
1 lime, juiced
2 tbsp soy sauce

Cut two squares of baking paper, then lay a fish fillet in the centre of each one. Scatter over the ginger, lemongrass, chilli and spring onions. Top with the pak choi, then pour over the lime juice and soy sauce. Scrunch up the parcels, place on a baking tray and bake at 200°C (180°C fan)/gas 6 for 20 minutes, until the fish is cooked through. Serves 2.

Leek

Leeks perform a similar role to onions, which is no surprise as they're part of the same family. With a white base and a fountain of green leaves, they're delicate and sweet in flavour and, like onions, are often found in a supporting role, whether sauteed, braised, griddled or slow cooked in the likes of soups, stews and gratins. Unlike onions, leeks grow above ground, so they tend to need a good wash; their funnel shapes make them mud traps, so split them in half and clean with cold water before cooking.

SEASON	Late summer to early autumn
PAIR WITH	Chicken, bacon, sausages, salmon, potatoes, peas, spring onions, squash, apples, chives, tarragon, butter beans, parmesan, ricotta, yoghurt, white wine, walnuts, lemon.
HACK	Save the tougher green leaves for making stocks, or use to wrap a bouquet garni to flavour soups.

Green lasagne

150g kale
1 tbsp olive oil, plus extra for drizzling
3 large leeks, chopped
1 large courgette, grated
1 garlic clove, chopped
250g ricotta
1 lemon, zested
200ml stock
3 tbsp pesto
Handful basil, leaves torn
250g fresh lasagne sheets
30g parmesan, grated

Layer leeks, courgette, kale and pesto in this fresh, lemony lasagne.

Bring a pan of salted water to the boil and cook the kale for 2 minutes, then drain. Heat the oil in a pan, then add the leeks, courgette and some salt and pepper and cook for 10 minutes. Stir in the garlic, cook for a minute, then add the cooked kale, ricotta, lemon zest, stock, pesto and basil. Spoon a quarter of the sauce into the bottom of a baking dish, top with lasagne sheets, then repeat until the ingredients are used up, finishing with a layer of sauce. Scatter with the parmesan, drizzle with oil and bake at 200°C (180°C fan)/gas 6 for 25 minutes. Serves 4.

Glamorgan sausages

3 leeks, sliced
2 tbsp olive oil
150g caerphilly or cheddar, grated
Small handful chopped parsley
Small handful chopped chives
1 tsp wholegrain mustard
250g fresh breadcrumbs
1 egg, beaten
1 tsp paprika

These Welsh vegetarian sausages are sure to cosset and hug. They are traditionally made with caerphilly, but you could also use cheddar.

In a large pan, cook the leeks with a pinch of salt in the oil for 10 minutes. Remove from the heat, stir through the cheese, herbs, mustard, 150g of the breadcrumbs, half the egg and some black pepper. Shape into eight sausages. Mix the remaining breadcrumbs with the paprika. Roll the sausages in the remaining egg then the breadcrumbs. Transfer to a baking tray lined with greaseproof paper. Chill in the fridge for at least 30 minutes, then bake at 200°C (180°C fan)/gas 6 for 30 minutes. Serves 4.

Quick leek and bean minestrone

2 tbsp olive oil
2 leeks, sliced
1 stick celery, diced
2 garlic cloves, crushed
700g jar white beans, drained
1 litre stock
1 lemon, zested and juiced
1 tbsp pesto
Large handful parsley, chopped
Grated parmesan, to serve (optional)

This is a good place to add any other greens you might have lying around, such as broccoli, peas or green beans. If you do, up the pesto to 2 tbsp.

Heat the oil in a large heavy-based pan, then add the leeks and celery and cook, stirring occasionally, until softened. Stir through the garlic, cook for a minute, then tip in the beans and stock. Simmer for 5 minutes, then add the lemon zest and juice, pesto and a good grind of black pepper. Cook for 2 more minutes, then stir through the parsley. Serve with handfuls of grated parmesan, if you like. Serves 6.

Leek and tomato rice

2 tbsp oil
3 leeks, sliced
1 garlic clove, chopped
150g cherry tomatoes, chopped
200g basmati rice
400ml stock
30g parmesan, grated
Large handful parsley, chopped

Baking is such a fail-safe way to cook rice, which is always harder to get right than it should be.

Heat the oil in an ovenproof pan, then cook the leeks with a pinch of salt until softened, about 8 minutes. Stir in the garlic, cook for a minute, then stir through the tomatoes, rice and a good grind of black pepper. Pour over the stock and bring up to simmering point. Combine the parmesan and parsley together in a bowl, then sprinkle this over the rice. Cover and bake at 220°C (200°C fan)/gas 7 for 30 minutes. Serves 4.

Leek, carrot and barley stew

2 tbsp olive oil
2 leeks, chopped
1 garlic clove, chopped
2 carrots, chopped
1 preserved lemon, flesh discarded, rind chopped
2 sprigs rosemary, leaves chopped
200g pearl barley
1 litre stock
Half a lemon, juiced

Satisfying and warming, this stew can be served as is for lunch, or with some chicken for dinner.

Heat the oil in a heavy-based pan, then cook the leeks with a pinch of salt for 8 minutes. Add the garlic, cook for a minute, then add the carrots, preserved lemon, rosemary and pearl barley. Tip in the stock, season and simmer for 45 minutes. Stir through the lemon juice. Serves 4.

Beetroot

Sweet, earthy beets are there no matter the weather, equally happy to turn their hand to warming curries in winter, as they are salads and dips come spring and summer. They range in size, with earthy notes becoming more prominent the bigger the roots get, as well as varieties: choose from purple, golden and candy-striped pink and white. Either way, they do need shaking up a bit to bring them to life, which could be done with salty capers, bitter greens, a mustard-based dressing or a sprinkling of deeply savoury chaat masala.

SEASON	Early summer to early spring
PAIR WITH	Sausages, mackerel, smoked salmon, white beans, goat's cheese, caraway seeds, chocolate, clementine, ginger, rhubarb, grapefruit, chaat masala, green beans, pomegranate, parsnips, labneh, carrots.
HACK	Don't let beetroot's habit of turning your fingers pink dissuade you: rubbing a piece of cut potato on your hands will (usually) make stains disappear.

Roast beetroot with labneh and raspberries

The labneh needs to drain overnight, so if time is an issue then use shop-bought instead.

1 tsp sea salt

500g natural Greek yoghurt

4 beetroot (about 850g), peeled and cut into small chunks

2 shallots, sliced

2 tbsp olive oil

2 sprigs thyme, leaves picked

100g raspberries

1 tbsp sherry vinegar

Mix the salt into the yoghurt, then put in a sieve lined with cheesecloth (or a clean J-cloth) set over a bowl; put in the fridge overnight. The next day, put the beetroot and shallots in an ovenproof dish, drizzle with the olive oil, add the thyme leaves and some salt and pepper and toss to coat. Bake at 220°C (200°C fan)/ gas 7 for 40 minutes. Meanwhile, in a bowl, crush the raspberries then mix with the vinegar. To serve, spoon the labneh onto a plate and top with the beetroot followed by the raspberries. Serves 4.

Beetroot, spring onion and feta muffins

This is a good moment to play around with flours; I've gone with spelt, but you could use wholemeal, or whatever needs using up.

100g beetroot, peeled and grated

3 spring onions, finely sliced

Half a lemon, juiced

70g self-raising flour

50g spelt flour

½ tsp baking powder

1 tsp chopped thyme leaves

50ml olive oil

80g natural yoghurt

1 egg, beaten

100g feta, crumbled

In a large bowl, combine the beetroot, spring onions, lemon juice, both flours, baking powder and thyme. In another bowl, mix the oil, yoghurt and egg, then stir into the beetroot mix. Crumble in the feta and season. Divide the mixture between six muffin cases, then bake at 200°C (180°C fan)/gas 6 for 30 minutes. Makes 6.

Beetroot and chocolate truffles

Beetroot and chocolate is a classic combo and really shines in truffles. These will keep in an airtight container in the fridge for 5 days.

200g dark chocolate, chopped

150ml double cream

20g butter

2 tbsp honey

60g cooked beetroot

Cocoa powder, for dusting

Put the chocolate in a heatproof bowl. Place the cream, butter and honey in a saucepan, then bring to just below boiling point. Pour the cream mix over the chocolate, stirring until smooth. Meanwhile, blitz the beetroot until smooth, then stir into the chocolate mix. Cover and put in the fridge to firm up, about 3 hours. Scoop out spoonfuls of the mix and roll into balls. Roll in the cocoa powder, shake off any excess, then return to the fridge. Makes about 16.

Beetroot and cherry gazpacho

This chilled soup is even better the next day, so make it ahead of time.

500g beetroot
400g tomatoes, halved
1 red pepper, chopped
Half a cucumber, chopped
1 small red onion, chopped
2 garlic cloves, peeled
3 tbsp olive oil
2 tbsp red wine vinegar
Handful cherries, halved
    and pitted

Cook the beetroot in salted boiling water until tender, about 45 minutes. Meanwhile, blitz the tomatoes, red pepper, cucumber, onion and garlic until you have a rough puree, then transfer to a bowl. Once the beetroot is cooked, drain and cool a little. Peel and chop then transfer to the food processor and blitz until smooth; transfer to the tomato bowl. Add the olive oil, vinegar and some seasoning, then combine and transfer to the fridge to chill. Serve topped with the cherries. Serves 4.

Beetroot borek

This simple pie can be made vegan by simply swapping the feta for a plant-based white cheese.

Olive oil
Small bunch spring onions,
    sliced
2 garlic cloves, crushed
Pinch of chilli flakes
1 lemon, zested
2 big handfuls spinach
700g beetroot, peeled
150g feta
60g walnuts, chopped
Big handful parsley, leaves
    chopped
6 sheets of filo
Nigella seeds, to sprinkle

Heat 1 tbsp oil in an ovenproof pan, add the onions and garlic and cook until softened. Add the chilli and lemon zest, then add the spinach and cook until wilted. Grate in the beetroot, stir, then crumble in the feta and add the walnuts, parsley and some seasoning. Transfer the mix to a bowl. Lay a sheet of filo in the base of the pan, slightly overhanging the edges, brush with a little oil, then repeat this process three more times. Tip in the beetroot filling, spreading it evenly across the base, then put the pan over a low heat and cook for about 4 minutes, to crisp the bottom of the pie. Fold in the overhanging filo, then scrunch the remaining filo and place on top. Brush with a little more oil, then sprinkle with nigella seeds. Bake at 200°C (180°C fan)/gas 6 for 30 minutes until golden. Serves 4-6.

Parsnip

With their starchy flesh, sweet, earthy parsnips are there when you crave comfort: mashed to top a pie, pureed into a silky soup, cooked down into dal or simmered for a slow braise. That said, giving this staple of the winter veg patch a good roasting is hard to better: soft, caramelized and achieving multiple textures in one fell swoop (thick at one end, wonderfully crisp at the other). Parsnips' sweet charms do, however, need taming and really benefit from being in the company of umami flavours, whether that's a spoonful of miso or a blanket of grated parmesan.

SEASON	Mid-autumn to early spring
PREP	Younger small parsnips don't need peeling, just give them a scrub; lightly peel older ones, then make a call on whether the core is too tough and needs removing.
PAIR WITH	Pork, chicken, cauliflower, carrots, potatoes, chestnuts, lentils, parmesan, mustard, nuts, honey, maple syrup, miso, harissa, apples, spices (nutmeg, turmeric, cumin, coriander), herbs (thyme, rosemary, sage).

Parsnip and harissa rosti

300g parsnips, grated
1 small shallot, finely sliced
1 egg, beaten
2 tbsp plain flour
1 tsp thyme leaves, chopped
1 tbsp harissa
1 tbsp olive oil

Everything is better with an egg on top and this rosti spiked with harissa is no exception.

In a large mixing bowl, combine the parsnips, shallot, egg, flour, thyme, harissa and some seasoning. Heat the oil in a large frying pan, then divide the parsnip mixture into six. Dollop three portions into the pan, flatten with a fish slice and cook until golden, about 6 minutes. Flip and cook on the other side for 5 minutes; transfer to a plate lined with kitchen towel. Cook the remaining rosti. Makes 6.

Parsnip gnocchi

400g parsnips, cut into large chunks
250g potatoes, cut into large chunks
1 egg yolk
100g plain flour, plus extra for dusting
40g parmesan, grated

This is a dream topped with sage and chopped hazelnuts cooked in melted butter.

Simmer the parsnips and potatoes in a pan of salted boiling water until tender, about 20 minutes. Drain and leave to steam dry. Once cool, tip them into a large bowl and mash until smooth. Add the egg yolk, flour and cheese and season with salt and a generous amount of black pepper. Turn out onto a lightly floured surface and knead until smooth. Divide into two, then roll each half into a log. Cut each log into 14 pieces and transfer to a floured plate. Cook the gnocchi in a pan of salted boiling water for 2-3 minutes, until they float to the surface. Drain on kitchen paper. Serves 4.

Miso-roast parsnips with tahini yoghurt

2 tbsp white miso
2 tbsp runny honey
2 tbsp olive oil
800g parsnips, quartered
250g natural yoghurt
2 tbsp tahini
1 lemon, juiced

The miso brings a good hit of umami to the sweet parsnips, all tempered by the tahini yoghurt.

In a small bowl, combine the miso, honey and oil. Put the parsnips on a baking tray, pour over the miso mix and toss to combine. Roast in a single layer at 200°C (180°C fan)/gas 6 for 45 minutes, stirring once or twice, until the parsnips are tender. Meanwhile, combine the yoghurt, tahini, lemon juice and a pinch of salt. Spoon the yoghurt onto a lipped dish and top with the sticky parsnips. Serves 4-6.

Parsnip and orange cake

150g unsalted butter
100g light brown sugar
1 orange, zested, plus the
   juice of half
3 eggs
200g parsnips, grated
200g plain flour
½ tsp baking powder
½ tsp bicarbonate of soda
1 tsp ground ginger
½ tsp grated nutmeg
1 tsp ground cinnamon
100g walnuts, roughly
   chopped
100g icing sugar

A good alternative to carrot cake, with all the usual suspects (cinnamon, walnuts, nutmeg). You could go for a cream cheese frosting, but for me a simple orange icing is just the ticket.

In a large bowl, cream together the butter, sugar and orange zest. Beat in the eggs one at a time, then mix in the grated parsnips. In another bowl, combine the flour, baking powder, bicarb and spices. Mix the wet ingredients into the dry ingredients until just combined, then stir through the walnuts. Pour the batter into a lined 22cm round cake tin and bake at 180°C (160°C fan)/gas 4 for 45 minutes, until a skewer inserted into the middle of the cake comes out clean. Remove from the oven, leave to cool in the tin for 15 minutes, then turn out onto a wire rack and leave to cool completely. Meanwhile, combine the orange juice and icing sugar. Once the cake is cool, drizzle over the icing and leave to set. Serves 10-12.

Parsnip dal

2 tbsp coconut oil
1 red onion, finely sliced
2 garlic cloves, crushed
Thumb-sized piece of
   ginger, finely chopped
1 red chilli, finely chopped
1 tsp ground turmeric
1 tbsp garam masala
200g dried red lentils
400ml coconut milk
500ml stock
4 parsnips (about 500g),
   grated
Half a lime
Large handful coriander
   leaves, chopped

Few things comfort and cosset quite like dal and you can never have too many in your repertoire. Eat with rice and quick-pickled veg.

Heat the oil in a heavy-based pan, then cook the onion, garlic, ginger and chilli until soft – about 10 minutes. Stir in the spices, cook for a minute, then tip in the lentils, coconut milk and stock. Bring to a simmer, add the grated parsnips and cook, stirring occasionally, for 30 minutes. Remove from the heat, add a good squeeze of lime juice and stir in the coriander leaves. Serves 6.

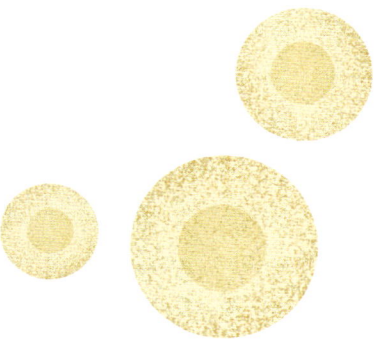

Lettuce

By 'lettuce', I really mean salad leaves – not just the sweet and crisp little gems, butterhead and the like, but peppery watercress and rocket, bitter red radicchio and fleshy chicory, too. When I was younger, the idea of cooking lettuce seemed odd – that was, until my mum came across a pasta recipe in which sliced little gems (and peas, I think) were stirred through at the end. Nowadays, I prefer the bitter side and am more likely to add shredded radicchio to short, stubby pasta shapes with mushrooms or sausages. Watercress, meanwhile, is reserved for soups (with pear), quiches and risottos; while those little gems now find themselves braised or put on the barbecue (as well as in a salad).

SEASON	All year round
VARIETIES	You have options: little gems are so soft they can be eaten raw or grilled; crisp, slightly bitter chicory and its blushing cousin radicchio are eaten raw (an excellent vehicle for dips) or grilled; peppery watercress is good in salads or soups, while rocket is perfect for topping pizzas and blitzing into pesto.
HACK	Little gems can masquerade as bread, cradling whatever filling you might otherwise pack between two slices.

Tofu laab in little gem cups

Oil
2 shallots, sliced
1 garlic clove, grated
Small thumb-sized piece
  of ginger, grated
1 red chilli, chopped
150g firm tofu, chopped
1 lime, juiced
1 tbsp soy sauce
Handful coriander leaves,
  chopped
Handful mint leaves,
  chopped
2 little gem lettuces,
  leaves separated

If you prefer, try swapping tofu for mince, whether that's chicken or pork.

Heat a little oil in a frying pan and cook the shallots, garlic, ginger and chilli for a few minutes, then tip in the tofu, 2 tbsp water and a pinch of salt. Cook on a high heat for 10 minutes, stirring to break up the tofu. Add the lime juice, soy sauce and herbs and toss well. Pile onto lettuce leaves to serve. Serves 2-4.

Sausage and chicory orecchiette

200g dried orecchiette
Olive oil
1 shallot, sliced
1 garlic clove, sliced
1 red chilli, chopped
4 sausages
1 tsp fennel seeds
Half a lemon, zested
  and juiced
100ml stock
1 chicory, leaves sliced

Scoop into bowls and serve under a blanket of grated parmesan.

Cook the pasta in salted boiling water according to packet instructions. Meanwhile, heat a glug of olive oil in a frying pan then cook the shallot, garlic and red chilli until softened. Remove the sausages from their skins, then add the meat to the pan, breaking it up with a spoon. Cook for about 5 minutes, until the meat is no longer pink, then stir in the fennel seeds and lemon zest. Pour in the stock and simmer until the liquid has reduced. Add the chicory, cook until wilted, then stir in the pasta and lemon juice. Serves 2-3.

Roast fennel, orange and radicchio salad

3 fennel bulbs, sliced
2 tbsp olive oil, plus extra
  for drizzling
1 radicchio
1 tbsp white wine vinegar
1 tsp honey
1 tsp wholegrain mustard
1 orange, juiced

Bitter radicchio leaves are balanced with the sweetness of roasted fennel and orange.

Put the fennel in a roasting tin with a drizzle of oil and some seasoning. Toss, then roast at 200°C (180°C fan)/gas 6 for 30 minutes. Meanwhile, break the leaves from the radicchio, tear into pieces and put in a serving bowl. In a small bowl, mix the olive oil with the vinegar, honey, mustard and orange juice and some salt and pepper. Pour over the radicchio, toss well, then add the fennel and toss again. Serves 4.

Tomato and watercress galette

125g plain flour, plus extra
for dusting
125g wholemeal spelt flour
120g butter, cubed
50g gruyère, grated
80g watercress,
roughly chopped
2 garlic cloves, chopped
Half a lemon, zested
and juiced
2 tbsp olive oil, plus extra
for drizzling
500g tomatoes, sliced
1 tbsp wholegrain mustard
Beaten egg, to glaze

Be sure to patch up any tears in the pastry before baking, to avoid spillage.

In a large bowl, combine the flours with a pinch of salt. Rub in the butter with your fingertips, then add the cheese. Pour in enough ice-cold water, a tablespoon at a time, to bring the dough together, then shape into a disc, wrap in clingfilm and chill for at least an hour. Meanwhile, put the watercress, half the garlic, the lemon zest and juice and the olive oil in a blender and blitz until smooth. Season and set aside. In a bowl, toss the tomatoes with the remaining garlic, mustard and a pinch of salt. Roll the chilled pastry out on a lightly floured worktop to the size of a dinner plate, then transfer to a lined baking sheet. Spread the base with the watercress mix, leaving a 2cm border. Tip the tomatoes over the watercress, then lift the pastry border up around the filling and pleat the sides. Brush the pastry with a little beaten egg, then drizzle the tomatoes with oil and bake at 200°C (180°C fan)/gas 6 for 45 minutes. Serves 6.

Braised lettuce with mushrooms

Olive oil
2 little gem lettuces, halved
100g mushrooms, chopped
1 garlic clove, crushed
1 sprig thyme, leaves picked
50ml stock
Sherry vinegar

If you eat meat, try frying bacon in a little veg oil, lift it out and use the remaining fat to cook the lettuce.

Heat a cast-iron pan and add a glug of oil. Season the lettuce halves then, once the oil is hot, add them to the pan cut-side down. Cook until charred, then remove the lettuce from the pan. Add the mushrooms to the pan and fry until crisp, then stir through the garlic and thyme. Return the lettuce to the pan with the stock, cover and simmer for 5 minutes. Add a splash of sherry vinegar and serve. Serves 2-3.

Jerusalem artichoke

These knobbly underground tubers, which are part of the sunflower family, are wonderfully earthy, meaning they're often destined to be blitzed into soups or — and this is perhaps my favourite way — incorporated into a creamy risotto. Jerusalem artichokes also roast sweetly, and they crisp up well too, rivalling any potato (although they're very happy to sit alongside them in a mash). They are, therefore, a prime candidate for making crisps, ideal for crumbling over soups or just snacking on with a cocktail.

SEASON	Mid-autumn to early spring
PAIR WITH	Pork, smoked haddock, shellfish, leeks, mushrooms, truffles, chestnuts, horseradish, hazelnuts, rosemary, paprika, cider, lemon.
HACK	Once peeled, artichokes discolour quickly, so place in a bowl of water with a squeeze of lemon juice until you're ready to cook them.

Gnocchi with Jerusalem artichokes, hazelnuts and sage

Jerusalem artichokes and potatoes are firm friends, and never so much as in this moreish yet light gnocchi dish.

2 tbsp olive oil
10g sage leaves
1 onion, thinly sliced
200g Jerusalem
  artichokes, diced
1 garlic clove, chopped
200ml stock
450g gnocchi
20g parmesan, grated
1 tbsp lemon juice
20g hazelnuts, toasted
  and chopped

Heat the oil in a large pan and, once hot, fry the sage leaves until crisp; scoop out and put on a plate lined with kitchen paper. Return the pan to the heat, then add the onion and Jerusalem artichokes and cook for 15 minutes. Stir in the garlic, cook for a minute, then tip in the stock and simmer until reduced by half. Cook the gnocchi according to packet instructions, then drain and stir into the veg pan. Add the parmesan, lemon juice and some black pepper, then serve topped with the hazelnuts and sage. Serves 2-3.

Jerusalem artichoke and paprika crisps

You want to slice the artichokes as thinly as possible, so use a mandolin if you have one.

300g Jerusalem artichokes
1 tbsp olive oil
1 tsp paprika
½ tsp fennel seeds, crushed

Slice the Jerusalem artichokes thinly, then transfer to a lined baking tray. Drizzle with the oil, add the spices and season. Toss well to coat, then spread in a single layer and bake at 220°C (200°C fan)/gas 7 for 30-35 minutes, until golden and crisp.

Roast Jerusalem artichokes with caraway, honey and feta

A simple side or turn into a salad with handfuls of watercress.

600g Jerusalem
  artichokes, cut into
  2cm pieces
1 tbsp olive oil
1 tsp caraway seeds
1 tbsp honey
30g feta

Put the Jerusalem artichokes in a baking dish, add the oil, caraway seeds and some seasoning, and toss well. Roast at 180°C (160°C fan)/gas 4 for 40 minutes, then stir in the honey and continue roasting for 5 minutes. Serve sprinkled with feta. Serves 4.

Jerusalem artichoke risotto

Here, the Jerusalem artichoke appears in two ways: roasted in chunks for texture, and blitzed for creaminess.

500g Jerusalem artichokes, cut into bite-sized pieces
Olive oil
1 litre stock
1 onion, diced
1 stick celery, diced
1 garlic clove, chopped
200g risotto rice
100ml white wine
Half a lemon, zested and juiced
30g parmesan, grated
Small handful basil, torn

Spread the Jerusalem artichokes out on a baking tray, drizzle with a little oil, season and toss to coat. Roast at 180°C (160°C fan)/gas 4 for 45 minutes, until golden. Transfer half to a food processor and blitz with 2 tbsp stock until smooth. Heat 1 tbsp oil in a large pan, then add the onion and celery and cook until tender – about 10 minutes. Add the garlic, cook for a minute, then stir in the rice to coat. Tip in the wine and simmer until it has evaporated. Start adding the stock a ladleful at a time, letting it absorb before adding the next. Continue until the rice is tender, about 30 minutes. Remove from the heat and stir in the pureed Jerusalem artichokes, roast Jerusalem artichokes, lemon zest, cheese and some black pepper. Add a good squeeze of lemon juice, then serve scattered with the basil. Serves 2–4.

Jerusalem artichoke and thyme soup

Serve topped with the artichoke and paprika crisps opposite (or just regular crisps).

1 tbsp olive oil
1 shallot, thinly sliced
1 leek, thinly sliced
1 garlic clove, chopped
2 sprigs thyme, leaves picked
700g Jerusalem artichokes, cut into chunks
100ml white wine
700ml stock

Heat the olive oil in a large pan, then add the shallot, leek, garlic, thyme and some salt and pepper and cook, stirring now and again, for 5 minutes. Add the Jerusalem artichokes and cook for 20 minutes. Pour in the wine, let it bubble away, then pour in the stock and simmer for 20 minutes. Blitz until smooth. Serves 4.

Rhubarb

A vegetable masquerading as a fruit, with crimson or green stalks depending on the time of year. The pink forced variety adds much-needed vibrance to the mellow months of January and February; its arrival also signals baking is imminent, perhaps cooked under a rubble of crumble or turned into a tart with its partner in crime, custard. While sugar, honey or maple syrup are required to bring welcome relief to rhubarb's sharp ways, it is this characteristic which also makes the vegetable appropriate for savoury things. Try it in a traybake with chicken or pork chops, roasted and eaten with pan-fried mackerel, lean into its crunch with a salsa or simmer down into chutney (with ginger and cardamom, for example) to eat with curries.

SEASON	The bright pink forced variety is available mid-winter to early spring, while the outdoor, more muted green stuff arrives in spring and is around until early summer.
PREP	Remove the leaves (they contain oxalic acid which, in quantity, is poisonous), wash the stalks, trimming the top and bottom. If you have a stash, chop it up and freeze in a single layer. Once frozen, tip into a container or bag.
PAIR WITH	Pork, chicken, lamb, mackerel, salmon, potatoes, chard, orange, blood orange, lime, strawberries, apples, pistachios, ginger, cardamom, star anise, sumac, vanilla, honey, elderflower, white chocolate, custard, booze (vodka, gin, champagne).

Rhubarb, ginger and white chocolate flapjacks

150g rhubarb, cut into 1cm pieces
150g unsalted butter
50g soft brown sugar
3 tbsp golden syrup
200g jumbo oats
3 balls of stem ginger (about 50g), chopped
1 tsp ground ginger
90g white chocolate, chopped

Rhubarb's sour snap means it's perfectly suited to warming ginger and sweet, creamy white chocolate.

Turn on the oven to 170°C (150°C fan)/gas 3. Put the rhubarb on a baking tray and into the oven as it heats. In a saucepan, melt the butter, sugar and golden syrup, then stir in the oats, stem and ground ginger and a pinch of salt. Remove from the heat, then leave to cool a little. Remove the rhubarb from the oven and, once cool, add to the oat mix with the white chocolate. Tip into a lined 20cm square baking tin, smooth the top and bake for 30 minutes, until golden. Once cool, cut into squares. Makes 12.

Chicken, rhubarb and potato traybake

500g new potatoes, halved
1 red onion, cut into 6 wedges
2 tbsp olive oil
1 tbsp honey
1 tbsp cider vinegar
2 bay leaves
200g rhubarb, cut into 5mm pieces
4 skinless and boneless chicken thighs

A simple Sunday lunch alternative, where the rhubarb breaks down almost to a sauce. Eat with greens, such as kale.

Put the potatoes, red onion, oil, honey, cider vinegar and bay leaves in a baking tray and season well. Toss everything together, then cover with foil and roast at 220°C (200°C fan)/gas 7 for 15 minutes. Remove the foil and stir through the rhubarb. Season the chicken thighs, then arrange on top of the veg and return to the oven for 30 minutes, until the chicken is cooked through and the potatoes are golden and tender. Serves 2.

Rhubarb, pistachio and cardamom scones

220g plain flour, plus extra for dusting
1 tsp baking powder
50g unsalted butter, cubed
40g caster sugar
1 tsp ground cardamom seeds
150ml buttermilk
1 tsp vanilla extract
60g pistachios, chopped
150g rhubarb, diced
Beaten egg, to glaze

The mix is quite sticky, so it's worth dipping your cutter in flour before stamping out the scones.

Add the flour, baking powder and a pinch of salt to a large mixing bowl. Rub in the butter until the mix looks like fine crumbs, then stir in the sugar and cardamom. Pour in the buttermilk and vanilla, mix with a knife, then stir through the pistachios and rhubarb. Turn the mixture out onto a lightly floured surface, knead briefly, then stamp out 6 round scones. Brush with beaten egg, then transfer to a lined baking tray. Bake at 200°C (180°C fan)/gas 6 for 20 minutes, until risen and golden. Makes 6.

Baked rhubarb with blood orange and star anise

400g rhubarb, cut into 3cm pieces

1 blood orange, zested and juiced

2 tbsp honey

1 star anise

This gives you options: pile onto porridge or pancakes for breakfast, or simply serve with yoghurt for a snack or dessert (ideally sprinkled with pistachios).

Put everything on a baking tray, toss together, then spread into one layer. Cover with foil and bake at 200°C (180°C fan)/gas 6 for 15 minutes. Remove the foil, shake the tray a little, then return to the oven for 5 minutes, until the rhubarb is tender but retains its shape. Serves 4.

Rhubarb ketchup

Glug of sunflower oil

500g rhubarb, chopped

1 small onion, diced

2 garlic cloves, finely chopped

Thumb-sized piece of ginger, chopped

2 bay leaves

1 tsp coriander seeds, crushed

100ml cider vinegar

50g caster sugar

Dollop this tart condiment into a bacon sandwich or serve alongside sausages or roast veg. This will keep in the fridge for a couple of weeks.

Heat the oil in a heavy-based pan, then add the rhubarb, onion, garlic, ginger, bay and some salt and pepper and stir well. Cook for 5 minutes until softening, then stir in the coriander seeds and continue cooking for 1 minute. Tip in the cider vinegar, 150ml water and the sugar and simmer for 15 minutes. Remove the pan from the heat, discard the bay leaves and leave to cool for 5 minutes. Blitz until smooth, then transfer to a sterilized jar.

Celeriac

Knobbly on the outside, snow white on the inside, celeriac is now one of my favourites of the root family – but that wasn't always the case. It used to be the vegetable that haunted my fridge, that was until I realized just how versatile it is, with its talents extending way beyond being grated or cut to use in salads or a remoulade with a dab of mustard (although they're good, too). When celeriac is cooked, that's when its sweetness really shines, bringing a velvety creaminess to soups and gratins.

SEASON	Mid-autumn to early spring
PAIR WITH	White fish, mackerel, scallops, smoked trout, pork, apples, pears, potatoes, parsnips, carrots, parmesan, comté, cream, horseradish, caraway, tahini, gochujang, thyme, hazelnuts.
HACK	Next time you're making mash, sub in half celeriac. Chop into chunks, boil for 5 minutes with the potatoes, then mash with your usual suspects.

Celeriac and tahini dauphinoise

1 large celeriac, finely sliced
1 large onion, finely sliced
2 garlic cloves, chopped
2 sprigs thyme, leaves
  picked and chopped
500ml hot stock
100g tahini
40g parmesan, grated

Technically this isn't really a dauphinoise because no cream is involved, but that's not to say it doesn't have the same comforting qualities.

Put the celeriac, onion, garlic and thyme in a bowl and season. Toss the lot together, then tip into a baking dish. Combine the hot stock and tahini, then pour over the celeriac mix. Cover with foil and bake at 200°C (180°C fan)/gas 6 for 1 hour, until tender. Scatter over the parmesan, then return to the oven for a further 30 minutes. Serves 4.

Gochujang celeriac steaks

1 celeriac, cut into
  4 thick steaks
1 tbsp gochujang
2 tbsp soy sauce
1 tbsp mirin
1 tbsp honey
2 tsp sesame oil

Here, you want a good-quality gochujang (fermented Korean red pepper paste) to add punch to the mellow celeriac steaks.

Score both sides of each celeriac steak and put in a large baking dish. In a bowl, combine the remaining ingredients, then tip over the celeriac. Toss well, then put in the fridge for an hour to marinate. Heat the oven to 200°C (180°C fan)/gas 6 and cook the steaks for 20 minutes, then flip them over and continue cooking for 10 minutes until tender. Serves 4.

Celeriac and sardine grain bowl

150g celeriac, shredded
1 apple, shredded
Large handful parsley, chopped
100g cooked puy lentils
2 x 120g tins sardines in olive oil, drained

FOR THE DRESSING
50ml olive oil
Half a lemon, juiced
2 tbsp natural yoghurt
2 tsp English mustard

I always have a couple of pouches of cooked puy lentils in the cupboard, ready for easy lunches and dinners. They work particularly well here, but you could always boil dried lentils.

In a large bowl, combine all the dressing ingredients. Add the celeriac, apple and parsley and toss to coat. Mix in the puy lentils and some salt and pepper, then roughly break in the sardines. Serves 2-4.

Celeriac and rosemary chips

1 large celeriac, cut into thick chips
2 tbsp vegetable oil
1 heaped tsp chopped rosemary

Don't have rosemary? Try thyme or sage instead.

Blanch the celeriac in salted boiling water for 2 minutes, then drain and leave to steam dry for 10 minutes. Tip the celeriac back into the pan and toss with the oil, rosemary and a big pinch of salt. Tip the lot onto a baking tray and put in the oven at 220°C (200°C fan)/gas 7 for 35-40 minutes, until crisp. Serves 4.

Celeriac, comté and sage fritters

1 celeriac, grated
1 garlic clove, finely chopped
80g comté, grated
1 tsp wholegrain mustard
Handful sage leaves, chopped
1 egg, beaten
30g flour
Oil, for frying

This is the kind of fritter to stuff inside a burger bun. I use plain flour, but you could also sub in gram flour or whatever needs using up.

In a large bowl, combine all the ingredients, except the oil, and season with salt and pepper. Shape into eight patties, then transfer to the fridge for 1 hour. Drizzle a little oil in a non-stick frying pan. Once hot, fry the patties for 4 minutes on each side, until golden - you will need to do this in batches. Makes 8.

Sweet potato

I came late to sweet potatoes, only previously having them in chip form (they were never *quite* crisp enough) and mashed to top pies, whether mince, lentil or otherwise. But their satisfying texture means they should be destined for so much more. As in life, though, you need contrast, so tame the soft, sweet nature of sweet potatoes with salty and spicy things, warming spices or fresh herbs. One thing to note, though, is that not all sweet potatoes are made equal; there are numerous varieties, with skin and flesh ranging in colour from tan to deep purple, and different textures and tastes.

SEASON	Mid-autumn to early spring
PAIR WITH	Pork, minced beef, salmon, mushrooms, avocado, spring onions, feta, chilli, ginger, lemongrass, coconut, pecans, pistachios, coriander, thyme, cinnamon, paprika, lentils.
HACK	Roasted sweet potato brings a welcome earthy flavour to bakes, too. Try roasting them in their skins, then scooping out the flesh and adding to a ginger cake batter.

Gigantes plaki with sweet potato

2 tbsp olive oil
1 onion, diced
1 garlic clove, finely
  chopped
1 stick celery, diced
1 sweet potato, peeled and
  chopped small
Pinch of ground cinnamon
Pinch of dried oregano
1 bay leaf
2 tsp tomato puree
400g tin chopped
  tomatoes
200g jarred butter beans,
  drained
100g feta
Large handful parsley,
  chopped

Eat at room temperature as part of a bigger spread, or spoon on top of toast for brunch.

Heat the oil in an ovenproof pan, then add the onion, garlic, celery and sweet potato and cook, stirring occasionally, until softened – about 10 minutes. Stir in the cinnamon, oregano, bay, tomato puree and chopped tomatoes and season with salt and black pepper. Simmer for 15 minutes, then tip in the beans with 150ml water and bring back to a simmer. Cover and transfer to the oven at 200°C (180°C fan)/gas 6 for 25 minutes. Remove from the oven, crumble over the feta and return to the oven uncovered for 5 minutes more. Scatter with the parsley and serve. Serves 4.

Sweet potato and red onion toad

150g plain flour
3 eggs
200ml milk
6 sausages
2 small sweet potatoes,
  cut into wedges
2 red onions, quartered
2 sprigs rosemary,
  leaves chopped
4 sprigs thyme,
  leaves picked
  and chopped
2 garlic cloves, chopped
Olive oil

It's important not to open the oven while the batter is cooking, otherwise it will collapse. A jug of onion and ale gravy (see page 59) on the side would be a very good thing.

Put the flour into a large bowl and whisk in the eggs. Gradually whisk in the milk, then season with salt and pepper and set aside. Put the sausages, sweet potato, onion, herbs and garlic in an ovenproof dish. Drizzle with olive oil, season and mix to coat. Put in the oven at 220°C (200°C fan)/gas 7 for 20 minutes, then remove from the oven, pour over the batter and cook again for 20–25 minutes until puffed up and golden. Serves 4.

Baked sweet potatoes with zhoug

Large bunch coriander, roughly chopped

Large bunch flat-leaf parsley, roughly chopped

2 green chillies, roughly chopped

1 tsp ground cumin

1 tsp ground coriander

1 lemon, juiced

4 tbsp olive oil, plus extra for drizzling

2 sweet potatoes

A few dollops of hummus

Using shop-bought hummus turns this into the ultimate easy sofa dinner (or working-from-home lunch).

Put the first seven ingredients in a food processor, add a pinch of salt and blitz until smooth; set aside. Scrub the sweet potatoes and prick all over with a fork. Put on a baking tray, drizzle with a little oil and sprinkle with salt. Bake at 180°C (160°C fan)/gas 4 for 1 hour, until you can pierce the potatoes easily with a knife. Cut each potato in half, add a couple of dollops of hummus and spoon over the zhoug. Serves 2.

Sweet potato and miso soup

Olive oil

2 small onions, finely chopped

3 garlic cloves, finely chopped

Thumb-sized piece of ginger, finely chopped

1 tsp ground turmeric

700g sweet potatoes, peeled and cut into small chunks

1 tbsp white miso

900ml stock

As it's velvety smooth with a good umami punch, you'll want to keep a few portions of this in the freezer. Your future self will thank you.

Heat a good glug of oil in a large saucepan, then cook the onion until softened. Add the garlic, ginger and turmeric and cook until soft. Add the sweet potatoes, miso and stock and bring to a simmer. Cover and cook for 30 minutes, until the sweet potatoes are soft. Blitz with a hand blender, then season. Serves 4.

Roast sweet potato and tahini dip

2 sweet potatoes, peeled and cut into chunks

Olive oil

1 tsp paprika

2 garlic cloves, chopped

2 tbsp tahini

1 lime, juiced

200g jarred white beans, drained

As far as I'm concerned, you can never have too many dips in your arsenal (or fridge), ready to turn toast, grains or salads into a meal.

Put the sweet potatoes on a baking tray, drizzle with oil, add the paprika, garlic and a pinch of salt and mix well. Roast in the oven at 200°C (180°C fan)/gas 6 until soft (about 40 minutes), turning halfway through; leave to cool. Tip into a food processor, add the tahini, lime juice and white beans and blitz until smooth. With the motor still running, add 2 tbsp oil and 2 tbsp water. Serves 6.

Fennel

First cultivated in Italy in the 17th century, this bulbous veg offers real bang for your buck. The dill-like fronds can be used as a garnish (like you would herbs), in salads or salsa verde; the stalks like celery for, say, a mirepoix; and the heart for frying. With its wonderful aniseed flavour, you can slice fennel thinly or shave raw for salad days with olive oil and citrus or yoghurt and a big handful of herbs. Alternatively, slice and serve up as crudites or juice the stalks and use in a vinaigrette. Much like onions, when you apply heat, fennel's sweet prowess emerges, making it ideal for roasting and sauteing for pastas and risottos or accompanying pork or oily fish.

SEASON	Mid-autumn to mid-spring
PAIR WITH	Mackerel, sardines, trout, hot-smoked salmon, anchovies, sausages, pork, lamb, beetroot, tomatoes, rocket, apples, dates, citrus, olives, mozzarella, parmesan, yoghurt, gochujang.
HACK	If you've got a lot of fennel fronds to use, chuck them in a blender with anchovy fillets, parmesan, garlic, lemon zest and juice and pistachios or pine nuts for a pesto.

Roast sausages with fennel and orange

4 sausages, pricked
1 red onion, sliced
1 fennel bulb, halved and
  finely sliced
1 orange, zested and juiced
1 sprig rosemary, leaves
  finely chopped
2 tsp Dijon mustard
1 tbsp olive oil
1 tsp fennel seeds

Let the oven do the heavy lifting with this throw-it-together traybake, ready in under an hour.

Put the sausages, onion and fennel in a large baking tray. In a bowl, combine the orange juice and zest, rosemary, mustard, oil, fennel seeds and some seasoning. Tip this over the sausages and veg and combine. Roast at 200°C (180°C fan)/gas 6 for 50 minutes, until the sausages are cooked through. Serves 2.

Fennel and lemon risotto

2 tbsp olive oil
2 fennel bulbs, finely sliced,
  fronds reserved
1 onion, diced
1 garlic clove, crushed
140g risotto rice
150ml white wine
700ml hot vegetable stock
1 lemon, zested, plus the
  juice of half
30g parmesan, grated
Knob of butter

Consider fennel fronds a bonus; treat them like herbs and use to garnish the risotto just before serving.

Heat the oil in a heavy-based pan, then cook the fennel and onion with a pinch of salt until softened, about 10 minutes. Add the garlic, cook for a minute, then add the rice and continue cooking and stirring for another minute. Pour in the wine and cook until it has been absorbed, then start adding the hot stock a ladleful at a time, stirring until it has been absorbed before adding more – this will take about 25 minutes. Remove from the heat, stir in the lemon zest and juice, cheese, butter and plenty of black pepper. Serve sprinkled with fennel fronds. Serves 2.

Quick-pickled fennel and cucumber

2 fennel bulbs, halved and
  finely sliced
1 red onion, finely sliced
1 large cucumber, halved,
  watery middle scooped
  out and the flesh
  finely sliced
1 tsp fennel seeds, crushed
3 tbsp cider vinegar
1 tsp caster sugar
Small handful tarragon,
  chopped

This quick pickle is even better served the next day, with grilled fish, pork chops or a grain salad.

Put all the ingredients apart from the tarragon in a bowl, season and scrunch together with your hands; set aside for 30 minutes. Stir through the tarragon. Serves 6.

Fennel, carrot and apple slaw

2 carrots, julienned
1 fennel bulb, finely sliced
1 apple, julienned
1 small onion, finely sliced
4 tbsp natural yoghurt
1 tbsp tahini
1 tsp sumac
Half a lemon, zested
  and juiced
1 garlic clove, crushed

The real joy of slaw is its adaptability. Success, however, comes down to a healthy combination of dressing and crunch. You can make this up to a day ahead.

Put the carrots, fennel, apple and onion in a large bowl and toss together. In a small bowl, combine the remaining ingredients, then tip over the veg. Give everything a good stir. Serves 4-6.

Fennel and saffron orzo

3 fennel bulbs, quartered
3 tbsp olive oil
1 shallot, finely diced
200g dried orzo
100ml white wine
500ml stock
Pinch of saffron

A little saffron goes a long way, with a pinch giving this easy weeknight meal a wonderful golden hue.

Put the fennel in an ovenproof dish, pour over 2 tbsp olive oil, season with salt and pepper and toss to coat. Pour in 100ml water, then bake at 200°C (180°C fan)/gas 6 for 30 minutes, stirring halfway through. Meanwhile, heat the remaining 1 tbsp oil in a heavy-based pan and cook the shallot until soft, about 10 minutes. Tip in the orzo, stirring to coat for a minute, then pour in the wine and continue cooking until the liquid evaporates. Pour in the stock, sprinkle over the saffron, season with black pepper and bring to the boil. Cook for 10 minutes, stirring occasionally to prevent the pasta from sticking. Divide between two bowls and top with the fennel. Serves 2.

Ginger

Ginger (alongside garlic and chilli) is the backbone of so many things I cook – grated into marinades, pickled and eaten with rice, preserved in syrup to chop and toss into tarts, dried and ground for chutneys or cookies, or sliced to float in boiling water with turmeric and lemon juice when a cold is brewing. Whichever way you cut it, this root's warming, gentle heat is a real powerhouse and sure to liven things up.

SEASON	All year round
PAIR WITH	Chicken, beef, pork, salmon, prawns, sea bass, tofu, aubergines, mushrooms, broccoli, pak choi, spring onions, rhubarb, apples, plums, pineapple, chilli, lemongrass, honey.
HACK	The easiest way to peel ginger is with a teaspoon, pressing the edge of the spoon against the root and pulling down.

Good morning shot

Large thumb-sized piece of ginger, chopped
1 apple, chopped
Half a lemon, zested and juiced

You could also add a pinch of ground turmeric, if the mood takes you.

Put all the ingredients in a blender with a splash of water and blitz. Strain through a sieve set over a glass and drink. Serves 1.

Apple and root ginger cake

200g plain flour
1 tsp baking powder
1 heaped tsp ground cinnamon
200g butter, melted
150g light muscovado sugar
2 large eggs
60g ginger, sliced
2 apples, cut into chunks

This is the kind of cake to have with a cup of tea. It will keep in an airtight tin (or well wrapped) for 2 days.

Put the flour, baking powder, cinnamon and a pinch of salt in a bowl and combine. Whisk together the melted butter and sugar, then add the eggs one at a time, mixing well after each addition. Fold the butter mix into the flour mix, followed by the ginger and apples. Tip into a greased and lined 22cm springform cake tin and bake at 190°C (170°C fan)/gas 5 for 45 minutes, until a skewer inserted into the middle comes out clean. Serves 8-10.

Soy and ginger salmon

Thumb-sized piece of ginger, finely chopped
1 garlic clove, finely chopped
2 tbsp soy sauce
1 tbsp rice wine vinegar
1 tsp sesame oil
Drizzle of honey
2 salmon fillets
1 spring onion, finely sliced
Sesame seeds, to serve

Eat with rice or noodles, plus some steamed or stir-fried pak choi.

Put the ginger, garlic, soy sauce, vinegar, oil and a drizzle of honey in a bowl and mix well. Add the salmon, toss to coat and set aside for 10 minutes. Transfer the lot to a baking tray, scraping out all of the marinade, and bake at 200°C (180°C fan)/gas 6 for 15 minutes. Serve topped with spring onion and sesame seeds. Serves 2.

Ginger, cashew and honey granola

60ml coconut oil, melted
60g honey
2 tsp vanilla extract
300g oats
50g pumpkin seeds
50g sesame seeds
40g ginger, grated
100g cashews,
  roughly chopped
80g sultanas

Store in an airtight container or jar for up to a month.

Combine the oil, honey and vanilla in a large bowl, then stir in the oats, seeds, ginger, cashews and a pinch of salt. Tip the lot onto a lined baking tray and bake at 180°C (160°C fan)/gas 4 for 30 minutes, stirring halfway through. Stir through the sultanas and, once cool, transfer to a jar or airtight container. Makes about 650g.

Pickled ginger

100g ginger, finely sliced
1 tsp salt
50ml rice wine vinegar
1 tsp sugar

This could be destined to eat with sushi or rice bowls, but it's also worth chopping up and tossing into stir-fries, too.

Put the ginger in a small bowl, stir in the salt and set aside for 30 minutes. Rinse the ginger with water then transfer to a sterilized jar. In a small saucepan, bring the vinegar, 100ml water and sugar to the boil. Pour over the ginger then leave to cool. Pop the lid on and leave for 48 hours before tucking in. Store for up to a month in the fridge. Serves 4–6.

Tomato

While technically fruits, tomatoes' affinity with savoury dishes makes them an honorary vegetable. They come in all shapes, sizes and colours, from sweet cherry tomatoes destined for salads and plum tomatoes for sauces, to big beefsteaks ideal for stuffing and green tomatoes for chutneys. What they all have in common, though, is they encapsulate the spirit of summer and when they're in their full glory, simple is often best: drizzled with oil and a pinch of salt, grated onto garlic-rubbed toast, finely chopped and marinated with garlic, herbs, vinegar and olive oil for a raw pasta sauce (because pasta salads are never acceptable).

SEASON	Early summer to mid-autumn
PAIR WITH	Anchovies, tuna, tofu, red peppers, kale, potatoes, aubergines, watermelon, chickpeas, cheese (feta, halloumi, manchego, mozzarella), miso, gochujang, tahini, harissa, bread.
HACK	If your tomatoes lack flavour, roast them - it intensifies their sweetness.

Roast tomato and miso sauce

800g tomatoes, halved
3 garlic cloves, crushed
2 tbsp olive oil
1 tbsp white miso
Pinch of chilli flakes
Large handful basil, torn

I mash the roast tomatoes with a fork (to save on the washing-up), but if you prefer a smoother sauce, blitz it.

Put the tomatoes in a roasting tin so they sit in a single layer (you may need two tins). In a small bowl, combine the garlic, oil, miso and chilli flakes, then season. Pour this over the tomatoes, toss, then roast at 190°C (170°C fan)/gas 5 for 1 hour. Crush the tomatoes with a fork until you have a smooth sauce, then stir through the torn basil. Serves 4-6.

Ratatouille and pistachio pesto tartlets

320g sheet puff pastry
3 peppers, sliced
1 red onion, cut into
    8 wedges
300g cherry tomatoes,
    halved
50g olives, roughly
    chopped
100ml olive oil, plus extra
    for the vegetables
200g pistachios
25g basil leaves
50g parmesan, grated
1 garlic clove, chopped
Half a lime, juiced

It's worth trying this pistachio pesto in other veg-based tarts, starting with butternut squash.

Unroll the pastry and cut into four equal rectangles. Score a 1cm border around each, then transfer to a lined baking tray; put in the fridge while you get on with the rest. In a large baking tin, toss together the peppers, onion, tomatoes, olives, 2 tbsp olive oil and some seasoning. Roast at 220°C (200°C fan)/gas 7 for 15-20 minutes, until softened. In a blender, pulse the pistachios, basil, parmesan, garlic and 100ml oil until you have a pesto. Add a good squeeze of lime. Remove the pastry from the fridge, then spread each base with pesto, leaving the borders clear. Top with the veg then return to the oven for 20 minutes until the pastry is puffed up and golden. Serves 4.

Tomato, gochujang and chickpea soup

1 onion, diced
2 garlic cloves, chopped
2 tbsp olive oil
500g tomatoes, chopped
1 tbsp gochujang
400g tin chickpeas, drained
300ml stock
Large handful parsley leaves, roughly chopped

The heat of gochujang varies, so give it a try before using. This soup has a kick to it, so if you prefer things on the milder side, halve the amount of gochujang.

In a heavy-based pan, cook the onion and garlic in the oil until soft, about 10 minutes. Add the tomatoes, cook for another 10 minutes, then stir in the gochujang, chickpeas, stock and some seasoning. Bring to the boil, then turn down the heat and simmer for a final 10 minutes, stirring through the chopped parsley. Serves 4.

Tofu, tomato and ginger scramble

300g silken tofu
1 tbsp oil
1 red onion, chopped
1 red chilli, finely chopped
Thumb-sized piece of ginger, grated
1 tsp cumin seeds, ground
½ tsp paprika
100g cherry tomatoes, chopped
Handful parsley leaves, chopped

Pile this onto hot toast or flatbreads. If you want to mix things up, add a handful or two of spinach with the tofu, stirring until wilted.

Put the tofu in a sieve over a bowl and leave to drain while you prepare the other ingredients. Heat the oil in a non-stick frying pan and cook the onion, chilli and ginger until soft, stirring occasionally, about 10 minutes. Add the cumin and paprika, cook for a minute, then stir in the tomatoes and a pinch of salt. Stir in the tofu, breaking it into pieces, and cook for 5 minutes until hot. Serve scattered with parsley. Serves 2.

Za'atar-roast tomatoes on whipped feta

300g cherry tomatoes, halved
2 garlic cloves, crushed
Olive oil
2 tsp za'atar
Handful parsley leaves, chopped
150g feta
3 tbsp natural yoghurt
Half a lemon, zested

While this is great for scooping up with bread, you could also serve this with drinks, spreading the feta onto crostini and topping with the tomatoes.

Put the tomatoes and garlic in a baking dish, season and drizzle with oil, then toss to coat. Roast at 180°C (160°C fan)/gas 4 for 40 minutes, then stir through the za'atar and parsley. Meanwhile, blitz the feta, yoghurt, lemon zest and a pinch of salt in a food processor until smooth. Spoon onto a plate, then top with the tomatoes. Serves 6 as a snack.

Squash

Squash is the reliable friend of the vegetable world: unassuming but comforting, brightening cool days with its perky sweetness. Coming in all manner of varieties, differing in colour, sweetness and density, they can on the whole be used interchangeably, so do experiment. Whichever you use, do keep in mind that the sweetness of squash can cloy, so it's best when paired with something savoury (think miso, bacon, parmesan) or with warming spices in, say, South Asian soups or Indian curries.

SEASON	Late summer to late autumn
PAIR WITH	Sausages, bacon, cheese (feta, blue cheese, parmesan, salted ricotta), cauliflower, spinach, mushrooms, radicchio, ginger, chilli, lemongrass, sage, dill, rosemary, orange, dates, coconut, pine nuts, hazelnuts, peanuts, chestnuts, honey, miso, soy sauce, harissa, chickpeas, lemon, vinegar.
HACK	Squash is your greatest ally in creating an instant, creamy sauce, especially in one-pot pasta dishes. Grate in the flesh towards the end of cooking.

Squash with anchovies and beans

1 small squash, peeled and cut into chunks
Olive oil
1 onion, sliced
3 garlic cloves, sliced
1 small glass of wine
1 rosemary sprig, leaves finely chopped
4 anchovy fillets
Pinch of chilli flakes
2 tsp tomato puree
325g jar butter beans, drained
60g parmesan, grated
Handful basil leaves, torn

This needs little more than some crusty bread, but you could make it into more of a meal by adding a green salad.

Put the squash in a baking dish, drizzle with oil and season well, then toss to coat. Roast at 200°C (180°C fan)/gas 6 for 30 minutes, until softened. In a large frying pan, heat a tablespoon of oil, then add the onion and cook until softened, about 10 minutes. Add the garlic, cook for a minute, then tip in the wine and cook until it has evaporated. Add the rosemary, anchovies and chilli flakes and cook for a couple of minutes, breaking up the fish with your spoon. Stir in the tomato puree, then tip in the cooked squash and beans and cook until heated through. Stir in the parmesan, season with salt and pepper, then serve topped with the torn basil. Serves 2.

Creamy squash and sage spaghetti

1 large squash, peeled and cut into chunks
2 garlic cloves, peeled
1 tsp dried sage
2 tbsp olive oil
200g dried spaghetti
25g parmesan, grated
Chilli flakes, to serve

The squash is roasted then pureed with pasta cooking water and parmesan to create an easy, creamy sauce.

Put the squash, garlic, sage and some salt and pepper on a baking tray. Drizzle over the oil, toss together and roast at 220°C (200°C fan)/gas 7, turning occasionally, for 45 minutes, until tender. Bring a large pan of salted water to the boil and cook the pasta according to packet instructions. Drain, reserving some of the cooking water. Once the squash is ready, transfer to a food processor and blitz with a mugful of the pasta cooking water and the parmesan, until smooth (alternatively, use a stick blender). Toss the pasta and sauce together until coated, adding a little more pasta cooking water to loosen, if needed. Serve sprinkled with chilli flakes. Serves 2, generously.

Braised eggs with squash, feta and za'atar

2 tbsp olive oil

3 leeks, sliced

200g peeled butternut squash, cubed

½ tsp cumin seeds, crushed

Half a lemon, zested

200ml stock

1 tsp za'atar

Small handful parsley, chopped

4 eggs

50g feta, crumbled

This works just as well for brunch as it does for dinner, with some sliced bread.

Heat the oil in a large saute pan for which you have a lid, then tip in the leeks, squash and some salt and pepper and cook, stirring occasionally, for 10 minutes until soft. Add the cumin, lemon zest and stock, then simmer for 5 minutes. Stir in the za'atar and parsley, then make four wells in the mix. Crack in the eggs, scatter over the feta, then cover the pan and cook until the whites are set but the yolks are still runny – about 5 minutes. Serves 2.

Squash, gruyère and mint pancakes

250g roasted butternut squash

1 egg

80g natural yoghurt

120g plain flour

1 tsp baking powder

30g gruyère, grated

5g mint leaves, chopped

Pinch of chilli flakes

Half a lemon, zested

Oil, for frying

Dressed rocket, to serve

An excellent place to put leftover roast squash to work. If you're making this from scratch, though, toss chunks of butternut squash with a little oil, season well and roast at 200°C (180°C fan)/gas 6 for 30 minutes.

Mash the squash in a large bowl, then whisk in the egg, yoghurt, flour and baking powder. Add the remaining ingredients (except the oil), season well and whisk again. Heat a little oil in a frying pan until smoking hot. Add spoonfuls of the mixture and cook for 2 minutes on each side, until golden. Serve topped with some dressed rocket. Makes 6.

Roast squash with paprika and rosemary crumb

1 large butternut squash (about 600g), peeled and sliced

4 tbsp olive oil

60g panko breadcrumbs

25g parmesan, grated

2 garlic cloves, crushed

1 tsp paprika

2 sprigs rosemary, leaves finely chopped

1 lemon, zested

A comforting butternut squash bake, crying out to be eaten with torn burrata.

Put the squash in a baking tray with 2 tablespoons olive oil and some seasoning and toss well. Roast at 200°C (180°C fan)/gas 6 for 35 minutes. Meanwhile, in a bowl, combine the breadcrumbs, parmesan, garlic, paprika, rosemary, lemon zest and the remaining 2 tablespoons olive oil. Scatter over the squash and return to the oven for 10 minutes. Serves 4.

Broad beans

Nothing says summer quite like the unzipping of these fluffy jackets. Whatever their age, broad beans always have a use; young pods can be eaten whole (and raw) with dips, while cooked beans should be tossed through salads, pastas and risottos, or served alongside the likes of grilled lamb. This is not the time to over-accessorize, mind, so let their brightness shine through; broad beans will live in harmony with spinach, lettuce and peas, as well as spices such as cumin and coriander.

SEASON	Early summer to early autumn
PREP	Double podding (removing the outer pod and the individual beans' casings) may seem like a faff, but it really is worth the effort – and if nothing else, it will keep idle hands occupied.
HACK	Freezing is the simplest solution to a glut of broad beans, with the pods perfect for future stocks and pre-blanched frozen beans ready for soups and risotto.

Broad bean, prawn and lime tartines

2 limes, zested and juiced
2 garlic cloves, crushed
Pinch of chilli flakes
Olive oil
150g peeled raw prawns
200g broad beans
2 slices soda bread

Tartines are the simplest vehicle for flavour – try this fresh, zingy combo for a late dinner with a glass of rosé.

In a large bowl, place half the lime zest and juice, the garlic, chilli flakes and a little olive oil. Add the prawns and set aside for 30 minutes. Meanwhile, blanch the broad beans in a pan of salted boiling water for 3 minutes, then drain and refresh under cold water. Tip into a food processor and add a glug of olive oil, the remaining lime zest and juice and some salt and pepper and blitz until smooth. Heat a griddle pan until hot, then cook the prawns until cooked through, turning once and basting with any marinade juices. Toast the bread, spread with the broad bean puree and top with the prawns. Serves 2.

Broad bean puttanesca with spaghetti

2 tbsp olive oil
1 red onion, finely sliced
2 garlic cloves, crushed
Big pinch of chilli flakes
1 tsp dried oregano
400g tin chopped
  tomatoes
100g black olives, chopped
1 tbsp capers, rinsed
300g broad beans
200g spaghetti, casarecce
  or orecchiette
Handful parsley leaves,
  chopped

Don't fancy pasta? Stir through a jar of butter beans instead, or pair the sauce with white fish.

Heat the oil in a frying pan, then add the onion and cook for 10 minutes, until softened. Stir in the garlic, chilli and oregano, cook for a few minutes, then tip in the tomatoes, olives and capers and bring to a simmer. In another pan, cook the broad beans in salted boiling water until tender, about 3 minutes; spoon into a bowl. When the beans are cool enough to handle, slip them out of their casings, stir into the sauce and keep over a low heat. Meanwhile, cook the pasta according to packet instructions, adding a splash of pasta cooking water to the sauce if it starts to look dry. Divide the cooked pasta between bowls, stir the parsley through the sauce and spoon over. Serves 2.

Broad bean pilaf

200g broad beans
200g basmati rice
1 tbsp olive oil
Knob of butter
3 shallots, finely chopped
1 garlic clove, finely chopped
300ml vegetable stock
Pinch of saffron
Handful dill, chopped

A fragrant pilaf that's equally good served as a main as it is an accompaniment to lamb.

Cook the beans in salted boiling water until tender, about 3 minutes. Drain and, when cool enough to handle, slip them out of their casings and set aside. Rinse the rice under cold running water, then soak in fresh water for 5 minutes. Meanwhile, heat the oil and butter in an ovenproof pan, then cook the shallots and garlic for 10 minutes, until softened. Tip in the rice, cook for a few minutes, then add the stock, broad beans, saffron and some seasoning. Cover and transfer to the oven at 200°C (180°C fan)/gas 6 for 20 minutes, until the liquid has been absorbed and the rice is cooked. Leave to rest for 5 minutes, then fluff with a fork and stir through the dill. Serves 2-4.

Braised eggs with broad beans and mint

2 tbsp olive oil
2 garlic cloves, crushed
1 large courgette, diced
1 lemon, zested
Small bunch spring onions, chopped
200g broad beans
Large handful mint, chopped
100ml stock
4 eggs
½ tsp sumac

Braised eggs are a good idea at any time of day - as long as there's bread and natural yoghurt on the side.

Heat the oil in a large frying pan, then add the garlic and cook for a minute. Add the courgette, lemon zest and some seasoning and cook for 15 minutes. Stir in the spring onions, broad beans, mint and stock and simmer for 5 minutes until most of the liquid has evaporated. Make four wells in the mixture, crack in the eggs, season and cover. Simmer until the whites are set but the yolks still runny, about 5 minutes, then sprinkle with the sumac. Serves 2.

Broad bean crab cakes

1 large potato (about 250g), peeled and cut into chunks
100g broad beans
Olive oil
1 shallot, finely chopped
1 garlic clove, chopped
Pinch of chilli flakes
200g crab meat
Handful parsley leaves, roughly chopped
½ tsp fennel seeds
1 lemon, zested
1 egg, lightly beaten
Flour, to dust

Serve these simple crab cakes with a good handful of watercress tossed with herbs and lemon juice.

Cook the potato in boiling water for 20 minutes, adding the broad beans for the final 3 minutes; drain and leave to steam dry. Once cool, transfer the lot to a large bowl and mash. Heat 1 tbsp oil in a frying pan and cook the shallot until softened. Add the garlic and chilli flakes, cook for a minute, then tip into the potato bowl. Mix in the crab, parsley, fennel seeds, lemon zest and egg, then chill in the fridge for 30 minutes. Shape into six patties, dust with a little flour on each side and fry in oil over a medium heat for 7 minutes per side, until golden brown. Serves 2-4.

Cabbage

Cabbage is the chameleon of the vegetable world, with the ability to transform into so many different dishes. A head of cabbage – whether crinkly, sweet savoy, red, green, pointed hispi, or the milder Chinese – can go a long way, and it has an impressively long shelf life to boot. That all said, it's taken me a while to warm up to the stuff (apart from my yearly batch of spiced red cabbage at Christmas, cooked until buttery soft). The turning point was the introduction of a hot grill, blistering the outside of wedges while the insides steam to crisp tenderness. And they're flavour magnets, soaking up whatever dressing you choose to pair with them (a lemony tahini one would be a good idea).

SEASON	Savoy: mid-autumn to late winter; red: late autumn to mid-winter; hispi: late spring to mid-autumn; white: midsummer to mid-winter; Chinese: late spring to early autumn
PAIR WITH	Savoy: chorizo, duck, anchovies, chestnuts, white beans, caraway; red: pork belly, apples, orange, carrots, cinnamon, star anise, port, pomegranate molasses, gochujang; hispi: chilli, tomatoes, tahini, hazelnuts, parmesan, yoghurt; Chinese: pork, prawns, red peppers, French beans, mint.
HACK	There's no better way to preserve Chinese cabbage than the fiery, fermented kimchi. Just a spoonful will pep up no end of dishes, from fried rice to toasties, and it's surprisingly easy to make.

Braised cabbage rolls

3 tbsp olive oil
2 red onions, sliced
2 garlic cloves, chopped
5 sprigs thyme, leaves picked
1 tbsp tomato puree
200g cooked rice
Small handful basil leaves, chopped
8 savoy cabbage leaves, central stem removed
100ml white wine
300ml stock

Be sure to remove the tough central stems from the cabbage leaves to make rolling easier.

Heat 2 tbsp of the oil in a pan, then cook the onions with some seasoning for 10 minutes. Stir in the garlic and thyme and cook for another few minutes. Stir in the tomato puree, followed by the rice and basil, then take off the heat. Bring a large pan of salted water to the boil and cook the cabbage leaves for 2 minutes; drain, refresh under cold water and pat dry. Divide the rice mix between the cabbage leaves, then roll each one up, folding in the sides to enclose the filling. Place the remaining oil in a large frying pan for which you have a lid, then add the stuffed cabbage parcels seam-side down. Pour over the wine, let it bubble away, then pour over the stock. Cover and leave to simmer for 25 minutes. Serves 4.

Okonomiyaki

2 eggs
50g flour
1 tsp soy sauce
1 tsp sesame oil
150g white cabbage, shredded
1 carrot, grated
2 spring onions, sliced
Oil, for frying

Serve this cabbage pancake with squirts of Japanese mayo and okonomiyaki sauce. If you don't have the latter, combine 2 tbsp ketchup with 2 tbsp Worcestershire sauce.

In a mixing bowl, whisk the eggs, flour, soy sauce, sesame oil and a pinch of salt. Fold in the cabbage, carrot and spring onions. Heat a little oil in a large frying pan then, once hot, spoon the cabbage mix into the pan, pressing down. Cook, covered, for 7 minutes, then flip the pancake onto a plate and slide it back into the pan the other way up. Cover again and cook for 6 more minutes. Serves 2.

Hispi salad with mint, almonds and pomegranate

1 hispi cabbage, shredded
60g almonds, toasted and chopped
150g pomegranate seeds
Small handful dill, chopped
Small handful mint, chopped
Small handful parsley, chopped
3 tbsp extra virgin olive oil
1 tbsp white wine vinegar
Half a lemon

My favourite way with hispi is to shred it into salads, with a load of herbs, fruit and nuts.

In a large bowl, combine the cabbage, nuts, pomegranate, herbs and a pinch of salt. In a jam jar, shake the olive oil, vinegar, a good squeeze of lemon juice and a pinch of salt. Taste and adjust if needed. Pour over the cabbage and toss well. Serves 4-6.

Red cabbage with apples and balsamic

1 red cabbage, shredded
1 onion, thinly sliced
Large pinch of allspice
200ml stock
50ml balsamic vinegar
2 apples, cut into chunks

This is particularly good at Christmas, but it works equally well on the side of any Sunday roast.

Put all the ingredients apart from the apples in a large pan, season, then simmer, stirring occasionally, for 30 minutes. Stir in the apples then continue cooking for 10 minutes. Serves 6.

Peanut cabbage noodles

Sesame oil
4 spring onions, chopped
Thumb-sized piece of
  ginger, chopped
1 garlic clove, chopped
Pinch of chilli flakes
250g savoy cabbage,
  shredded
2 nests of dried egg
  noodles
4 tbsp peanut butter
3 tbsp soy sauce
1 tbsp rice wine vinegar

Cabbage really welcomes bold flavours, which is why it works so well with this garlic, soy and peanut butter sauce.

Heat a little oil in a pan, then add the spring onions, ginger, garlic and chilli flakes and cook for 4 minutes. Add the cabbage and continue cooking for another 8 minutes – you want the cabbage to get a little charred. Meanwhile, bring a pan of water to the boil and cook the noodles according to the packet instructions. Drain, reserving a mugful of cooking water. In a small bowl, combine the peanut butter, soy sauce, rice vinegar and 1 tsp sesame oil. Tip the noodles and sauce into the cabbage pan, add 4 tbsp noodle cooking water and toss to coat well. Serves 2.

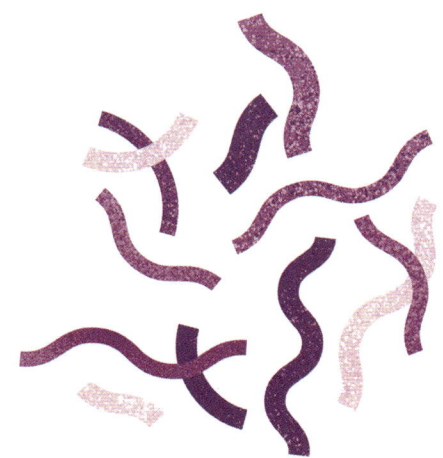

Celery

F. Scott Fitzgerald wrote, 'Never miss a party. Good for the nerves – like celery', and I couldn't agree more. The base of so many soups, stews, braises and sauces would be at a loss without the inclusion of a stick or two of this aromatic vegetable. That said, I don't think celery always gets the love it deserves. Slightly bitter with earthy notes, eaten raw (tossed into salads, dunked in dips, or just smeared with cream cheese), it's wonderfully crisp and fibrous. Cooking it (whether that's braised, in a stir-fry, or gratin) tones things down beautifully.

SEASON	Early autumn to late spring
PAIR WITH	Bacon, crab, tinned sardines, blue cheese, tomatoes, apples, grapes, chilli, tarragon, parsley, walnuts, kombu, peanut butter, lentils, turmeric, vinegar.
HACK	Don't forget celery leaves; treat them like herbs in a garnish for soups, or whizz into pesto.

Roast potatoes with bloody mary sauce

1kg new potatoes, halved
3 tbsp olive oil
1 shallot, diced
2 sticks celery, diced
1 garlic clove, chopped
1 tbsp vodka
400g tin cherry tomatoes
2 tsp Worcestershire sauce
¼ tsp celery salt
Dash of Tabasco
1 tbsp lemon juice

Roast potatoes are the perfect vehicle to carry this cocktail-inspired sauce.

Put the potatoes in a baking tray, toss with 2 tbsp olive oil and some seasoning, and roast at 200°C (180°C fan)/gas 6 for 45 minutes, shaking occasionally, until crisp. Meanwhile, heat the remaining 1 tbsp oil in a pan, then add the shallot and celery and cook for 10 minutes. Stir in the garlic, cook for a minute, then add the vodka and cook until evaporated. Add the tinned tomatoes, Worcestershire sauce, celery salt and a dash of Tabasco and simmer for 15 minutes, until thickened. Stir through the lemon juice. Tip the roast potatoes into a serving bowl and spoon over the sauce. Serves 4.

Celery and thyme soup

2 tbsp olive oil
1 leek, diced
1 onion, diced
6 sticks celery, diced
300g potatoes, diced
100ml wine
600ml stock
2 thyme sprigs,
  leaves picked
Half a lemon, juiced

Put aside some celery leaves to scatter over the soup just before you serve it.

Heat the oil in a heavy-based pan, add the leeks, onion, celery, potatoes and some seasoning, and saute for 10 minutes. Pour in the wine, let it bubble away until evaporated, then tip in the stock and thyme and bring to a simmer. Cook, covered, for 20 minutes, then transfer half of the veg to a bowl. Blitz the remaining veg using a hand blender in the pan until smooth, then tip the bowl of veg back in. Stir in the lemon juice and ladle into bowls. Serves 4-6.

Cashew and celery stir-fry

Oil
60g cashews
8 sticks celery, sliced on
  the diagonal
2 garlic cloves, grated
Thumb-sized piece of
  ginger, grated
1 red chilli, chopped
1 tbsp soy sauce
1 tbsp rice wine vinegar
1 tsp honey
4 spring onions, sliced

A speedy stir-fry to serve simply with rice, or on the side of fish.

Heat a glug of oil in a large pan, then fry the cashews until toasted, about 4 minutes; transfer to a plate. Add a little more oil to the pan, then cook the celery for 5 minutes. Stir in the garlic, ginger and chilli, cook for 5 minutes, then tip in the toasted cashews. Stir in the soy sauce, vinegar and honey, then serve scattered with the spring onions. Serves 2-4.

Celery Caesar salad

2 anchovy fillets, plus
  a little oil from the tin
80g natural yoghurt
2 tbsp olive oil
2 tbsp lemon juice
10g parmesan, grated
50g panko breadcrumbs
10 sticks celery,
  thickly sliced
Large handful parsley,
  leaves chopped

Celery takes the lead role in this classic salad. You could add a crushed garlic clove to the dressing, if you fancy.

In a small bowl, mash the anchovies, then combine with the yoghurt, olive oil, lemon juice, parmesan and some salt and pepper. Add a little oil from the anchovy tin to a pan and, once hot, tip in the breadcrumbs and toast, stirring, until golden and smelling biscuity. Season. Put the celery and parsley in a serving bowl, tip over the dressing and mix to coat. Serve topped with the breadcrumbs. Serves 4.

Lentil bolognese

1 shallot, chopped
1 large carrot, chopped
2 sticks celery, chopped
Pinch of chilli flakes
1 tbsp olive oil
200g chestnut
  mushrooms,
  chopped small
2 garlic cloves, chopped
2 sprigs thyme,
  leaves picked
1 bay leaf
1 tbsp tomato puree
400g tin chopped
  tomatoes
300g dried puy lentils
800ml stock
1 tbsp balsamic vinegar
Cooked pasta, to serve

This will keep in the fridge for 3 days, otherwise store in the freezer for up to 3 months.

Cook the shallot, carrot, celery and chilli flakes in the oil for 5 minutes, then add the mushrooms and cook for another 5 minutes. Add the garlic, thyme and bay, cook for a minute, then stir in the tomato puree. Tip in the tomatoes, lentils, stock and some black pepper, then simmer for 25 minutes. Finally, stir in the vinegar before spooning over cooked pasta. Serves 8.

Recipe index

Acknowledgements

Thank you to Skittledog and everyone involved in making *Vegetable Genius,* but particularly to Zara Larcombe and Virginia Brehaut. A big thank you to Joanna Smith for your eagle eye(s), and to Agnieszka Więckowska for the beautiful illustrations – they make the book. A special thank you to Ron and Keith for providing vegetables from their garden; to Jeannette, for all the recipe testing; to Alan, Tom and the various guinea pigs for always being hungry and offering opinions; and finally, to you, for buying this book.

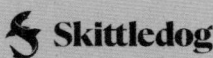 **Skittledog**

First published in the United Kingdom in 2025
by Skittledog, an imprint of Thames & Hudson Ltd,
181A High Holborn, London WC1V 7QX

Vegetable Genius © 2025 Thames & Hudson Ltd, London

Text © 2025 Anna Berrill
Illustrations © 2025 Agnieszka Więckowska

Senior Editor: Virginia Brehaut
Cover Designer: Alison Guile
Designer: Sarah Pyke
Production: Felicity Awdry

British Library Cataloguing-in-Publication Data
A catalogue record for this book is available from the British Library

ISBN 978-1-837-76036-7

Impression 01

Printed and bound in China by C&C Offset Printing Co., Ltd

INTERART S.A.R.L. (GPSR)
19 rue Charles Auray, 93500 Pantin, Paris
http://www.interart.fr/
productsafety@thameshudson.co.uk

Be the first to know about our new releases, exclusive content and author events by visiting:

skittledog.com
thamesandhudson.com
thamesandhudsonusa.com
thamesandhudson.com.au